UNITARIAN
UNIVERSALISM

Zondervan
Guide to Cults &
Religious Movements

ZONDERVAN
GUIDE to CULTS &
RELIGIOUS
MOVEMENTS

UNITARIAN UNIVERSALISM

ALAN W. GOMES
Author and Series Editor

ZONDERVAN™

GRAND RAPIDS, MICHIGAN 49530 USA

To my wife, Diane:
Encourager, fellow traveler on the way

ZONDERVAN™

Unitarian Universalism
Copyright © 1998 by Alan W. Gomes

Requests for information should be addressed to:

Grand Rapids, Michigan 49530

Library of Congress Cataloging-in-Publication Data

Gomes, Alan W., 1955 –
    Unitarian Universalism / Alan W. Gomes.
        p. cm. — (Zondervan guide to cults and religious movements)
    Includes bibliographical references.
    ISBN 0-310-48891-5 (softcover)
    1. Unitarian Universalist churches — Controversial literature. 2. Unitarian
Universalist Association — Controversial literature. I. Title. II. Series:
Zondervan guide to cults & religious movements.
BX9847.G58 1998
289.1 — dc21
                                                      97-33441
                                                           CIP

Interior design by Art Jacobs

Printed in the United States of America

---

98 99 00 01 02 03 04 05 /❖ DP/ 10 9 8 7 6 5 4 3 2 1

Contents

 # How to Use This Book

The *Zondervan Guide to Cults and Religious Movements* comprises fifteen volumes, treating many of the most important groups and belief systems confronting the Christian church today. This series distills the most important facts about each and presents a well-reasoned, cogent Christian response. The authors in this series are highly qualified, well-respected professional Christian apologists with considerable expertise on their topics.

We have designed the structure and layout to help you find the information you need as quickly as possible. All the volumes are written in outline form, which allows us to pack substantial content into a short book. With some exceptions, each book contains, first, an introduction to the cult, movement, or belief system. The introduction gives a brief history of the group, its organizational structure, and vital statistics such as membership. Second, the theology section is arranged by doctrinal topic, such as God, Christ, sin, and salvation. The movement's position is set forth objectively, primarily from its own official writings. The group's teachings are then refuted point by point, followed by an affirmative presentation of what the Bible says about the doctrine. The third section is a discussion of witnessing tips. While each witnessing encounter must be handled individually and sensitively, this section provides some helpful general guidelines, including both dos and don'ts. The fourth section contains annotated bibliographies, listing works by the groups themselves and books written by Christians in response. Fifth, each book has a parallel comparison chart, with direct quotations from the group's literature in the left column and the biblical refutation on the right. Some of the books conclude with a glossary.

One potential problem with a detailed outline is that it is easy to lose one's place in the overall structure. Therefore, we have provided graphical "signposts" at the top of the odd-numbered pages. Functioning like a "you are here" map in a shopping mall, these graphics show your place in the outline, including the sections that come before and after your current position. (Those familiar with modern computer software will note immediately the resemblance to a "drop-down" menu bar, where the second-level choices vary depending on the currently selected main menu item.) In the theology section we have also used "icons" in the margins to make clear at a glance whether the material is being presented from the group's viewpoint or the Christian viewpoint. For example, in the Mormonism volume the sections presenting the Mormon position are indicated with a picture resembling the angel Moroni in the margin; the biblical view is shown by a drawing of the Bible.

We hope you will find these books useful as you seek "to give an answer to everyone who asks you to give the reason for the hope that you have" (1 Peter 3:15).

—Alan W. Gomes, Ph.D.
Series Editor

# Foreword

Although there are not large numbers of Unitarian Universalists in the United States today, the influence of their worldview on law, education, politics, popular culture, and public policy is enormous. If you have ever been told that the Bible is mostly myth, morality is relative, believing in the exclusivity of Christianity is intolerant, abortion is a fundamental right, and human sexuality should be limited only by the choices of consenting adults, then you have been confronted by aspects of the Unitarian Universalist worldview.

Professor Alan Gomes, in this well-researched and clearly written volume, has given the church a resource that will help it to understand, critique, and dialogue with those who embrace the religious and philosophical perspectives of the Unitarian Universalist church.

There are some in the church who may not agree with Professor Gomes's approach. They may think that it is not worth our time to understand and study viewpoints that challenge the truth of Christianity. These well-meaning brethren often quote to support their case, without regard to context, the words of the apostle Paul: "See to it that no one takes you captive through hollow and deceptive philosophy" (Col. 2:8 NIV). This passage is no more telling Christians to stay away from studying non-Christian philosophies than a command to not drink poison is telling Christians not to be pharmacists. That is, one cannot discern the difference between bad and good philosophy without a grasp and understanding of different viewpoints. The practice of Paul on Mars' Hill (Acts 17) makes this quite clear. As C. S. Lewis once wrote in *The Weight of Glory*, "To be ignorant and simple now — not to be able to meet the enemies on their own ground — would be to throw down our weapons, and to betray our uneducated brethren who have, under God, no defense but us against the intellectual attacks of the heathen. Good philosophy must exist, if for no other reason, because bad philosophy needs to be answered."

Professor Gomes has given us good philosophy.

— Francis J. Beckwith, Ph.D.
Associate Professor of Philosophy, Culture, and Law
Trinity International University (Deerfield, Ill.),
California campus

 # Acknowledgments

Although many people have helped in the preparation of this book, a few stand out as particularly worthy of mention. Mr. Roland Dooley, my former student, assisted me greatly in the early stages of this project, hunting down and evaluating valuable resources. The staff at Biola University's Rose Memorial Library was exceptionally helpful, particularly Mr. Bob Krauss and Ms. Mary Gupta, who did outstanding work in securing crucial periodical information. Thanks go to Mrs. Cara Ender for her accurate and speedy transcription work. I also benefited much from the insightful comments and bibliographical suggestions of my good friends Bob and Gretchen Passantino of Answers in Action. Finally, I am grateful for the patience and support of my wife Diane and my boys, Colin and Trevor — not only shown in the production of this book but also demonstrated throughout the long hours I invested as general editor for this fifteen-volume series.

Part I: Introduction

I. What the Unitarian Universalist Association Is

A. **The Unitarian Universalist Association** is an association of fellowships, churches, or societies[1] that subscribe to certain broad principles and purposes and affiliate themselves organizationally with the UUA denomination, headquartered in Boston, Massachusetts.

B. **The names Unitarian and Universalist reflect the historical roots of the denomination.**

    1. Unitarian

        a. The Unitarians are so named because they denied the Trinity.

        b. The Unitarian movement with which we are concerned arose during the sixteenth-century Reformation.

        c. It spread from continental Europe (particularly Poland) to England and then to America.

    2. Universalist

        a. The term *Universalist* refers to the salvation of all human beings.

        b. The Universalists opposed the doctrine of eternal punishment, teaching instead that God would save each and every human being.

        c. In the eighteenth century, Universalist teachings spread from England to America.

    3. Merger of the Two Groups

        a. In America the Unitarians and Universalists developed cordial relationships, due to their similar beliefs and attitudes.

        b. The two groups merged officially in 1961, forming the Unitarian Universalist Association (UUA).

        c. Members of the Unitarian Universalist Association are often simply called "Unitarians."[2]

---

[1]John Sias from interviews with Rev. Steve Edington, *100 Questions That Non-Members Ask About Unitarian Universalism* (n.p.: Transition Publishing, 1994), 26–27.

[2]To avoid confusion, whenever I am speaking about a member of the Unitarian Universalist Association, I will describe that person as a "Unitarian Universalist," or a "UU" for short. Before the merger in 1961, the Unitarians and Universalists were organizationally separate. Therefore, in the history section I refer either to "Unitarians" or to "Universalists" as appropriate. Note, too, that the term *unitarian* (lower case) can be

4. The Unitarian Universalists should not be confused with the Unity School of Christianity or the Unification Church.[3]

C. *The UUA is pluralistic, meaning that the group tolerates and even encourages within its ranks a wide diversity of belief.*

1. For example, the UUA embraces theists, Neo-pagans, liberal "Christians,"[4] religious humanists, atheists, and more.

2. Because of this wide variation in belief, a simple statement of UUA theology and practice is not possible. Nevertheless, this book presents and critiques the main forms of belief and practice found in today's UUA. See especially Part II, Section I.B.

II. The Problem of Analyzing UUA Beliefs

A. *Factors Contributing to the Problem of Ascertaining UUA Beliefs*

1. The pluralism of the UUA makes it difficult to define their beliefs.

   a. Some UUs favor a particular faith stance (e.g., liberal "Christianity"), though not to the exclusion of other faith stances.[5] Other UUs mix and match different belief systems into one of their own.

   b. UUA pluralism makes classification and exposition of UU belief challenging. (See Part II, Section I.B.)

2. Because the Unitarian Universalists are noncreedal—even anticreedal—one cannot point to a specific statement of faith or systematic theology that speaks for the entire group.[6]

B. *Procedure Followed in this Book for Analyzing UUA Beliefs*

1. This book identifies the unity within the diversity of UUA beliefs.

   a. As one peruses UU writings, certain principles and beliefs often emerge, which can—at least generally—be taken as normative representations of current UUA belief and practice.

   b. I have consulted the most prominent and influential UUA authors. Because UU belief is a moving target, I have emphasized their most recent writings offered by their primary spokespersons (e.g., their president, denominational officials, influential clergy et al.).

---

used to describe anyone who holds to a unitarian view of the Godhead (e.g., Jehovah's Witnesses), whether or not they have any historical or organizational tie with the Unitarian Universalist denomination.

[3]For a thorough treatment both of the Unity School of Christianity and of the Unification Church, see Todd Ehrenborg, *Mind Sciences* (Grand Rapids: Zondervan, 1995), and J. Isamu Yamamoto, *Unification Church* (Grand Rapids: Zondervan, 1995), both in this series.

[4]In referring to UU "Christians," I do not wish to be misunderstood. As this book demonstrates, UUs are not Christian, whether they claim this for themselves or not. When used in the context of Unitarian Universalism, the label "Christian" is one of self-attribution only; I deny that it can truly apply to a Unitarian Universalist. (See Part II, Section I.C.8 below.)

[5]See, for example, Arvid Straube, "The Bible in Unitarian Universalist Theology," *The Unitarian Universalist Christian* 44, no. 1 (1989): 28.

[6]Though in this regard see Part II, Section I.B.2.d.

    c. I have paid close attention to UU works published by official UUA presses (e.g., Beacon Press, Skinner Books, the UUA itself).[7]

    d. Wherever possible, I have relied on UUs' own self-descriptions and analyses of their beliefs.

2. Even though *positive* UU belief is quite diverse, one finds considerable unanimity in their denial of historic Christian orthodoxy.

    a. Although UUs frequently disagree among themselves as to what they do believe, there is little doubt about what they *do not* profess. UUs completely reject the historic, biblical Christian teaching on such issues as the unique deity of Jesus Christ, his literal bodily resurrection, his role as the only Savior, atonement (satisfaction of God's wrath) through his blood, and other orthodox Christian doctrines.

    b. In their denials one often finds similar arguments. Thus, even though there is wide latitude in their beliefs, their arguments against historic, biblical Christianity are much less diverse.

III. Historical Background

A. *General Observations*[8]

1. The UUA traces its roots to the radical wing of the Reformation, which considered itself the true heirs of New Testament Christianity.[9]

2. Although never viewed as genuinely Christian by its orthodox foes, the UUA has seen itself as such until this century. Generally speaking, today's UUA does not claim Christian allegiance even though individual UUs and certain UU congregations do.

3. Historian Earl Morse Wilbur pointed out that as Unitarianism spread from Poland and Transylvania through Germany and Holland to England and America, the various manifestations of Unitarianism all claimed Christian allegiance.[10]

---

[7]Note that certain predominately UU publishers, such as Beacon, also publish non-UU works. I am speaking here of writings that are clearly UU in orientation.

[8]For a brief overview of Unitarian and Universalist history in chart form, see John A. Buehrens and F. Forrester Church, "A Brief Chronology of Unitarian Universalist History," in *Our Chosen Faith: An Introduction to Unitarian Universalism* (Boston: Beacon, 1989), 187–92.

[9]In the sixteenth century there were some who disagreed not only with Rome but also with the mainline reformers, feeling that men such as Martin Luther and John Calvin did not go far enough. These people were more "radical" in their rejection of traditional theology and practice, and hence are called "radical reformers" or leaders of the "radical reformation." Many (though not all) of the radical reformers rejected the orthodox doctrines of the Trinity and the two natures in Christ. See George H. Williams, *The Radical Reformation*, 3d ed. (Kirksville, Mo.: Sixteenth Century Journal Publishers, 1992).

[10]Earl Morse Wilbur, *History of Unitarianism*, 2 vols. (Boston: Beacon, 1945; Cambridge, Mass.: Harvard University Press, 1952), 1:4. See also Lloyd F. Dean, "The Withering of Unitarianism," *Gordon Review* 5, no. 1 (Spring 1959): 15. Although sometimes the connections are loose, the movements are related.

4. George Marshall notes that around the time of the Revolutionary War, "Unitarianism emerged first and most conspicuously from the Calvinistic First Parishes of the Congregational order, whereas Universalism emerged from the Methodist and Baptist churches."[11]

B. **Early Unitarianism in Continental Europe**

   1. Michael Servetus (1511–1553)[12]

      a. Many UUs consider Michael Servetus, a Spanish physician, the founder of their movement.[13]

      b. Among his most influential—and highly controversial—writings were his *De Trinitatis erroribus libri vii* of 1531 (*On the Errors of the Trinity in Seven Books*) and his *Christianismi Restitutio* of 1546 (*The Reconstitution of Christianity*).

      c. After escaping from the Catholics, Servetus made his way to Geneva to propagate his views, in spite of being warned sternly by Calvin not to set foot there.

      d. After a trial lasting some three months, he was burned alive at Champel on October 27, 1553.

      e. Servetus's execution generated sympathy for his cause and raised him to the stature of a martyr for his anti-Trinitarian faith.[14]

   2. Faustus Socinus (1539–1604), Socinianism, and the "Minor Reformed Church" in Poland

      a. The anti-Trinitarian party grew and was organized under the able leadership of Faustus Socinus, an Italian who migrated to Poland.[15]

      b. Socinus became the de facto leader of the so-called Polish Brethren, known officially as the Minor Reformed Church.[16]

      c. He championed their cause in writing and in oral debate, entering into disputes with the orthodox over cardinal doctrines such as the Trinity and the Atonement.[17]

---

[11]George N. Marshall, *Challenge of a Liberal Faith*, rev. enl. ed. (New Canaan, Conn.: Keats, 1980), 82. See also Mason Olds, "Religious Humanism and Unitarianism," *Religious Humanism* 12, no. 1 (1978): 15.

[12]See Roland H. Bainton, *Hunted Heretic: The Life and Death of Michael Servetus, 1511–1553* (Boston: Beacon, 1960).

[13]See, for example, Marshall, *Challenge of a Liberal Faith*, 15. Although some seek earlier antecedents (e.g., Arius), it seems more historically plausible to trace the roots to Servetus.

[14]Although some scholars consider Servetus to be a forerunner of modern Unitarianism, his doctrine is perhaps more accurately classified as a kind of tritheism. Wilbur even suggested that it might be considered a species of pantheism (*History of Unitarianism*, 1:209–10). Regardless, Servetus's critique of the Trinity was influential in Poland and in the movement led by Faustus Socinus (see III.B.2 below).

[15]The best comprehensive general history of Socinianism is Wilbur's previously cited, two-volume *History of Unitarianism*.

[16]Wilbur, *History of Unitarianism*, 1:328. Poland was the most religiously tolerant country of the day, as under King Sigismund (1540–1571), a Unitarian. See Church, "Deeds Not Creeds," in *Our Chosen Faith*, 58.

[17]See Alan W. Gomes, "De Jesu Christo Servatore: Faustus Socinus on the Satisfaction of Christ," *Westminster Theological Journal* 55 (1993): 209–31.

    d. Under Jesuit persecution, the Unitarians largely were forced out of Poland. Some merged with Unitarians in nearby Transylvania. Others migrated to the Netherlands, where Remonstrant (Arminian) and Mennonite congregations often received them hospitably.

    e. The Unitarian movement took firm root in Transylvania and Hungary and is still active there today.

C. Early Unitarianism in England

1. John Biddle (1615–1662) and English Unitarianism

    a. John Biddle is known as the father of English Unitarianism.

    b. The authorities arrested Biddle numerous times for spreading heretical views about the Trinity.

    c. Biddle's *Twelve Arguments Drawn out of Holy Scripture* and *A Confession of Faith Touching the Holy Trinity According to the Scripture* attempt to prove both from reason and from Scripture that the doctrine of the Trinity is illogical and unbiblical.

    d. In 1654 Oliver Cromwell sent him into exile on the Scilly Islands. He eventually died in prison (1662).

2. Theophilus Lindsey (1723–1808)

    a. Lindsey was an Anglican clergyman who left the Church of England over theological differences. He objected to the Book of Common Prayer's requiring him to worship Christ and the Holy Spirit.

    b. Lindsey became friends with Joseph Priestley,[18] with whom he cooperated in spreading the Unitarian cause.

    c. With Priestley's support, Lindsey established the Essex Street Chapel on April 17, 1774. Wilbur describes this as "the first place in England that came to anything, which was avowedly intended for the worship of God on Unitarian principles."[19]

    d. Benjamin Franklin frequented Lindsey's church while he stayed in England on business on behalf of the colonies.

    e. Lindsey wrote two books that set forth his view of the person of Christ, "the prevalent worship of whom he boldly attacked as no better than 'Christian idolatry.'"[20]

3. English Unitarianism in the Nineteenth Century

    a. Laws persecuting Unitarians were rescinded in the nineteenth century, enabling Unitarians to function and grow as a denomination.

    b. In 1825 the Unitarians formed the British and Foreign Unitarian Association, which made them more effective.

---

[18]See III.D.4 below.

[19]Earl Morse Wilbur, *Our Unitarian Heritage* (Boston: Beacon, 1925), 352; George N. Marshall, "Unitarian Universalism," in *Encounters with Eternity: Religious Views of Death and Life After-Death*, eds. Christopher Jay Johnson and Marsha G. McGee (New York: Philosophical Library, 1986), 295.

[20]Wilbur, *Our Unitarian Heritage*, 354.

    c. In the nineteenth century, Unitarianism moved in a more rationalistic direction under leaders such as James Martineau.[21]

D. American Unitarianism in the Eighteenth and Nineteenth Centuries

  1. General Observations

    a. In the seventeenth century, Unitarianism was strictly outlawed in the colonies.[22] It was not until the late eighteenth century that Unitarianism began to make inroads into the established churches.

    b. Particularly infected were the Congregational churches, which maintained their structure but adopted a Unitarian theology.

      (1) Most Congregationalists who apostatized to Unitarian theology were graduates of Harvard, which had become theologically liberal.

      (2) "In all, approximately 125 churches became Unitarian and either withdrew or were forced from the Congregational denomination."[23]

  2. Jonathan Mayhew (1720–1766)

    a. Mayhew was the minister of the West Church, Boston, from 1747 to 1766.

    b. Mayhew "preached against the Trinity in 1753, and two years later urged in print the strict unity of God. . . . he was the first preacher in America to come out squarely in speech and in print against the doctrine of the Trinity."[24]

  3. King's Chapel, Boston

    a. King's Chapel (Episcopal) in Boston was the first church in America to become officially Unitarian in its theology, though not in name.

    b. In 1785 the liturgy (e.g., Book of Common Prayer) was revised to omit references to the Trinity.

    c. In 1787 the church ordained James Freeman as minister and became "Anglican in worship, congregational in polity, and unitarian in theology."[25]

  4. Joseph Priestley (1733–1804)[26]

    a. Joseph Priestley is famous for both his religious views and his scientific contributions (e.g., studies in chemistry and electricity).

---

[21]Ibid., 384.

[22]See Wilbur, *Our Unitarian Heritage*, 391.

[23]Harry Scholefield and Paul Sawyer, "Our Roots," in *The Unitarian Universalist Pocket Guide*, ed. William F. Schulz, 2d ed. (Boston: Skinner House, 1993), 14.

[24]Wilbur, *Our Unitarian Heritage*, 396–97.

[25]Buehrens and Church, "A Brief Chronology," 189.

[26]On Priestley and his significance, see Joseph Henry Allen, *An Historical Sketch of the Unitarian Movement Since the Reformation* (New York: Christian Literature Company, 1894), 154–59.

    b. As Allen observes, Priestley "may be said almost alone to have shaped the system of opinion by which the Unitarianism of that period [i.e., the eighteenth century] is best known."[27]

    c. Priestley denied the Virgin Birth and Christ's sinlessness. However, he did believe in the miracles recorded in Scripture and considered them essential for the Christian faith. He also believed in the second coming of Christ and in the resurrection on the last day.[28]

    d. In 1794 Priestley left England for America because of persecution for his liberal views. Priestley was on friendly terms with Washington, Jefferson, Adams, and Franklin.

    e. Benjamin Franklin encouraged Priestley to start a church. In 1794, Priestley established the first Unitarian church in Northumberland, Pennsylvania. This church was the first that explicitly applied the name "Unitarian" to itself.[29]

    f. "[Priestley] together with Lindsey deserves to be regarded as one of the two modern founders of the movement that exists to-day."[30]

5. First Parish in Plymouth

    a. In 1620 the Pilgrims founded the First Parish Church in Plymouth.

    b. This church went over to Unitarianism in 1802, having called Rev. Nathaniel Kendall, a Unitarian, as its minister a year earlier.[31]

6. Harvard College

    a. Originally founded by Puritans in 1636, Harvard College eventually succumbed to Unitarian influence.

    b. Henry Ware, a Unitarian, was appointed to a chair of divinity in 1805, indicating the clout of liberals at Harvard.

    c. Other liberal appointments followed, including a liberal president.

    d. Andover Seminary opened in 1808 as a conservative alternative, in hopes of counteracting the growing liberalism at Harvard.

7. William Ellery Channing (1780–1842)

    a. Channing was arguably the greatest light of American Unitarianism. Robust and articulate, he was known as the "apostle of Unitarianism."

    b. Channing held that Christ was much more than a man but still less than God.[32]

    c. Channing's so-called Baltimore sermon, preached at the ordination of Jared Sparks in 1819, marks a watershed in the debate. (He entitled his sermon "Unitarian Christianity.")

---

[27]Ibid., 154.

[28]Wilbur, *Our Unitarian Heritage,* 367–68.

[29]Ibid., 404.

[30]Ibid., 368.

[31]Marshall, *Challenge of a Liberal Faith,* 79.

[32]Channing held to a kind of Arianism rather than Socinianism. See Conrad Wright, *The Beginnings of Unitarianism in America* (Boston: Beacon, 1955), 4, 201–2.

(1) In this famous sermon, Channing argued that the doctrine of the Trinity is unscriptural and irrational. He also charged that it caused one to be distracted in the worship of the one true God, who is a unity, not a confusing trinity of persons.[33]

(2) As historian Wilbur stated, "Probably no other sermon ever preached in America has had so many readers and so great an influence."[34]

d. Some leading orthodox thinkers of the day opposed Channing's views, including Moses Stuart of Andover and Dr. Lyman Beecher.

e. Channing actively engaged the social issues of his day. For example, he strongly opposed slavery.

8. Founding of the American Unitarian Association

a. The American Unitarian Association was founded May 25, 1825, by a dozen recent graduates of Harvard Divinity School.

b. Channing gave "passive approval" to the group but declined to be its first president.[35]

c. The new association received but muted enthusiasm. Wilbur attributed the lukewarm response to the Unitarian aversion to centralized denominational control, which many feared might lead to an undesirable uniformity of belief.

9. Ralph Waldo Emerson (1803–1882) and the Transcendentalists

a. Emerson and Henry David Thoreau were two particularly well-known transcendentalists.

b. Transcendentalism was an intellectual movement that captivated the minds of many of the literary elite in nineteenth-century America.

c. Transcendentalism "was an offshoot of Unitarianism, which many thought had become too conservative and orthodox, just as a century before Unitarianism had broken from Congregationalism because of the latter's supposed conservatism."[36] Most of those involved in the transcendentalist movement were Unitarians.

d. The transcendentalists placed their emphasis on religious intuitions rather than on reason or on the teachings or purported miracles of Jesus. God reveals his truths to us directly and inwardly.[37]

e. Transcendentalist teachings seemed to move toward pantheism.[38]

---

[33]William Ellery Channing, "Unitarian Christianity," in *Three Prophets of Religious Liberalism: Channing, Emerson, Parker,* introduction by Conrad Wright (Boston: Beacon, 1961), 60–62.

[34]Wilbur, *Our Unitarian Heritage,* 414. See also F. Forrester Church, "Neighborhood," in *Our Chosen Faith: An Introduction to Unitarian Universalism* (Boston: Beacon, 1989), 121.

[35]Wilbur, *Our Unitarian Heritage,* 420.

[36]Barry A. Kosmin and Seymour P. Lachman, *One Nation Under God* (New York: Harmony Books, 1993), 44.

[37]Wilbur, *Our Unitarian Heritage,* 433.

[38]Pantheism teaches that "God is all and all is God." That is, God is identical to his creation; God and the universe are identical.

  f. In 1838, Emerson delivered a controversial address to the divinity students at Harvard in which he bemoaned that few churches existed where "man [is] made sensible that he is an infinite Soul; that the earth and the heavens are passing into his mind; that he is forever drinking the soul of God."[39]

  g. Emerson's writings served as a conduit for Hindu and Eastern mystical beliefs.

  h. Both orthodox Christians and old-guard Unitarians attacked Emerson's views as "the latest form of infidelity."[40]

10. Theodore Parker (1810–1860)

  a. Emersonian thought influenced Parker.

  b. Parker became famous for his 1841 sermon entitled "The Transient and the Permanent in Christianity."

   (1) Though Parker did not deny the biblical miracles, he downplayed their importance and argued that Christianity would be true even if Christ himself had never existed and miracles had never occurred.[41]

   (2) Parker argued that while the *form* in which particular Christian doctrines may be expressed is transient, the underlying great truths that Jesus taught are permanent.

  c. Though Parker himself affirmed miracles, his depreciation of them contributed to their eventual denial by later generations.

11. The Free Religious Association (FRA) of 1867

  a. The more radical among the Unitarians started this association.

  b. The more conservative Unitarians wished to retain a professed allegiance to Jesus Christ and to continue to bear the name "Christian." The FRA urged a more inclusive posture.

  c. At the National Conference of 1868, members of the FRA secured an amendment to the constitution that allowed complete freedom of belief. Thus, earlier statements affirming Unitarians as disciples of Jesus, or Jesus as God's Son, were no longer binding.[42]

E. *American Universalism in the Eighteenth and Nineteenth Centuries*[43]

1. General Observations

  a. It is important to note that the Universalists originally developed their movement and churches separately from the Unitarians.

---

[39]Ralph Waldo Emerson, "The Divinity School Address," in *Three Prophets of Religious Liberalism,* 102.

[40]See John McClintock and James Strong, *Cyclopedia of Biblical, Theological, and Ecclesiastical Literature* (1867–1887; reprint, Grand Rapids: Baker, 1981), s.v. "Norton, Andrews."

[41]Theodore Parker, "The Transient and the Permanent in Christianity," in *Three Prophets of Religious Liberalism,* 133.

[42]Wilbur, *Our Unitarian Heritage,* 454–55.

[43]For an overview of Universalism in America see Ernest Cassara, ed., *Universalism in America* (Boston: Beacon, 1971), 1–44.

    b. The similar approaches of the Unitarians and the Universalists led to cooperation and their eventual merger (in 1961) under a single denominational umbrella.

    c. The famous Universalist Thomas Starr King quipped, "The Universalists believe that God is too good to damn them, whereas the Unitarians believe they are too good to be damned!"[44]

2. John Murray (1741–1815) and the First Universalist Church in America[45]

    a. Though not the first to preach it, Murray was perhaps the most important early advocate of universalism in America.[46]

    b. Murray migrated from England to America in 1770. Though originally a Methodist, Murray began preaching universalist doctrines.

    c. Murray and his fellow universalists could not reconcile the doctrine of hell with the notion of a loving God.

    d. In 1779 Murray founded the first Universalist church in America—called the "Independent Christian Church"—in Gloucester, Massachusetts.

3. Hosea Ballou (1771–1852)[47]

    a. In 1789 Hosea Ballou converted to universalist ideas. He first espoused these in a supposedly "Calvinistic" sense of "election," teaching—contra Calvin—that the entire human race was "elect."[48]

    b. Ballou eventually rejected even this modified form of "Calvinism," but continued to advance universalistic teachings.

    c. Ballou abandoned the Bible's teaching on original sin, the Trinity, substitutionary atonement, and hell.[49]

    d. Ballou was pastor of the Second Universalist Church in Boston from 1817 until his death.

    e. Ballou was a tireless advocate of universalism, a prolific author, and the editor of two magazines.[50]

F. *Rise of Humanism Among the Unitarians*[51]

1. John H. Dietrich and Curtis W. Reese: Founders of Early Humanism

    a. Just after the turn of the century, a philosophy known as "humanism" arose among certain Unitarians.

---

[44]Buehrens, "Experience," in *Our Chosen Faith*, 34.

[45]See Cassara, *Universalism in America*, 10–14.

[46]For example, Charles Chauncy (1705–1787) and George de Benneville (1703–1793) preached universalistic doctrines before Murray arrived on the scene. See Cassara, *Universalism in America*, 6–9.

[47]Ibid., 17–24.

[48]*Encyclopedia Britannica*, on-line edition, s.v. "Ballou, Hosea."

[49]Original sin is the teaching that we are guilty and morally corrupt because of Adam's sin (see Part II, Sections V.C.2 and V.D.2 below). Substitutionary atonement is the idea that Jesus bore the punishment for our sins in our place, as our substitute.

[50]*Encyclopedia Britannica*, on-line edition, s.v. "Ballou, Hosea."

[51]For this discussion, I am particularly indebted to Olds, "Religious Humanism and Unitarianism."

   b. This new philosophy bred considerable controversy between humanist and theist Unitarians, notably between 1918 and 1937.

   c. Rev. John H. Dietrich coined the term *humanism*. Curtis W. Reese, minister of the Des Moines Unitarian Church, was presenting a very similar form of teaching as "the religion of democracy." Eventually, humanism won out as the label for the teaching.

   d. The main theses of this teaching are that "people are the rulers of their own affairs"; people must solve their own problems rather than seeking divine assistance; "human welfare" rather than the "glory of God" is the proper aim of religion; and religion should focus on "this worldly" concerns rather than on an age to come.[52]

   e. Reese dared to suggest that liberals need not be dogmatic about whether God even existed.[53]

   f. The controversy came to a head in 1921 at the Western Unitarian Conference in Detroit. The theists failed to pass a resolution making belief in God a requirement for Unitarians.

2. The *Humanist Manifesto I* of 1933

   a. This document revived the controversy within the Unitarian ranks.

   b. As Ed Doerr notes, half of the signers of the 1933 *Humanist Manifesto I* were Unitarian Universalist ministers, as were the first four presidents of the American Humanist Association and other notable participants.[54]

   c. The manifesto also had the support of John Dewey, the famous philosopher and educator, and "a score of Unitarian ministers."[55]

   d. Kurtz and Bullough summarize the manifesto as follows: "The *Manifesto* called for a new statement of the purposes of religion. It held that the universe was self-existing rather than created, and that humans are a part of nature and a product of evolution. It urged the use of science and reason, rather than supernatural beliefs, to explain natural phenomena. It maintained that human values could not be derived from theistic doctrines or expectations of salvation. Values arise from human communities, and the highest value is the complete realization of human personality and the quest for the good life here and now."[56]

3. Eventually, the theists and humanists managed to coexist within Unitarianism because of the emphasis on freedom of thought.

---

[52]Olds, "Religious Humanism and Unitarianism," 16.

[53]Ibid., 19, quoting Reese.

[54]Ed Doerr, "Book Reviews: *The Quality of Religious Life in Unitarian Universalist Congregations: A Survey by the Commission on Appraisal* and *Our Chosen Faith: An Introduction to Unitarian Universalism,*" *The Humanist* (May/June 1990): 45.

[55]Paul Kurtz and Vern L. Bullough, "The Unitarian Universalist Association: Humanism or Theism?" *Free Inquiry* 11, no. 2 (Spring 1991): 12–13.

[56]Ibid. See also Dean, "The Withering of Unitarianism," 22.

4. The American Humanist Association of 1943

   Edwin Wilson, a Unitarian minister, founded this association and became the editor of the association's *Humanist* magazine.

5. "Religious" vs. "Secular" Humanism

   a. Wilson regarded himself as a "religious" rather than a "secular" humanist. He believed that words such as "God," "religion," and "religious" should be applied to humanistic and naturalistic concepts.[57]

   b. Other humanists, however, objected to using such religious terminology in that the labels would tend to confuse.

   c. In 1980 the Council for Democratic and Secular Humanism was founded, inserting the adjective "secular" in their name to distinguish themselves from the "religious" humanists.[58]

6. In 1989 a UUA survey of its membership showed that at least two-thirds of all members considered themselves to be some flavor of humanist.[59] But it does appear that humanism's influence is declining within the UUA.[60]

G. The Unitarian Universalist Association (UUA)

1. In 1961 the American Unitarian Association (AUA) and the Universalist Church of America (UCA)[61] merged to form the Unitarian Universalist Association (UUA).

2. The headquarters for the UUA is in Boston, Massachusetts.

3. The UUA continues to become more liberal, as shown by some significant decisions made since 1970:

   a. 1970—The UUA ordains homosexuals to ministry.

   b. 1984—The UUA decides to perform "ceremonies of union" for gay and lesbian couples.

   c. 1985—Sexist and patriarchal language is expunged from the UUA hymnbook.

   d. 1985—The Covenant of Unitarian Universalist Pagans (CUUPS) affiliate organization is constituted at the General Assembly.

   e. 1988—The UUA General Assembly adopts a "right to die" resolution.[62]

   f. 1996—UUA General Assembly becomes the first denomination to officially advocate the legalization of same-sex marriages.[63]

---

[57]Kurtz and Bullough, "The Unitarian Universalist Association: Humanism or Theism?" 12–13.

[58]Ibid., 13.

[59]Unitarian Universalist Association, *The Quality of Religious Life in Unitarian Universalist Congregations: A Survey by the Commission on Appraisal* (Boston: Unitarian Universalist Association, 1989), 31, 46.

[60]See V.B.1 below.

[61]Formerly known as the Universalist General Convention (UGC).

[62]"Unitarians Support Doctor-Assisted Suicide," *Washington Post,* 7 July 1990, sec. C.

[63]"Unitarians Endorse Same-Sex Marriages," *Los Angeles Times,* 29 June 1996, Home Edition, Metro section.

IV. Vital Statistics

A. *Membership Figures*

1. Official UUA Membership Statistics

   a. The official membership rolls show 211,597 registered members of the UUA in 1,034 congregations worldwide.[64]

   b. The UUA is virtually an American phenomenon: Officially, 204,046 Unitarians reside in the United States, with 6,528 in Canada.

   c. Massachusetts, the UU mecca, boasts the largest concentration, with a total of 34,696 registered UUs in 146 congregations.[65]

2. Unofficial Statistics

   a. The total number of Americans who consider themselves UUs far outstrips the number who have signed the membership roster.

   b. In 1990, researchers Barry A. Kosmin and Seymour P. Lachman did a very accurate survey of religious affiliation across the continental United States.[66] According to this survey, about 502,000 Americans consider themselves Unitarian Universalists—over twice the number published by the UUA.[67]

   c. This means that UUs number nearly as many as Muslims in the United States (527,000) and significantly more than Buddhists (401,000)—groups that draw more attention from missiologists.[68]

3. Growth Trends[69]

   a. In the mid-1960s, official UUA membership was around 250,000 and steadily declined for 17 years, to a low of 166,000 in 1980. Since 1981 the trend has reversed and membership has grown.[70]

   b. Based on official UUA statistics, the UUA is now growing at a rate of about 4 percent per year[71]—its largest growth in twenty years.

---

[64]*Unitarian Universalist Association 1997–98 Directory* (Boston: Unitarian Universalist Association, 1997), 58.

[65]Ibid., 39. Note that non-UUA Unitarians are found in other parts of the world, particularly in Romania (80,000) and in Great Britain (10,000). Although organizationally distinct, these foreign groups maintain some contacts with the UUA.

[66]Kosmin and Lachman surveyed 113,000 people across the continental United States. This computer-generated survey represents "the largest and most comprehensive poll ever on religious loyalties, and the most accurate and detailed as to geographical distribution" (*One Nation Under God,* 2). It is important to note that this study measured religious *self-identification;* it indicates how the respondents viewed themselves, regardless of whether they officially joined the particular church in question.

[67]Ibid., 16.

[68]Ibid.

[69]See V.A below regarding the UUA's recent efforts at outreach.

[70]Chandler, "Unitarians: Oneness in Diversity," 20.

[71]*UUA 1995–96 Directory* (Boston: Unitarian Universalist Association, 1995), n.p.

B. *Demographics*
1. The social status and prestige of Unitarian Universalists is noteworthy. Russell Chandler observes that the UUA has "exerted influence far greater than its numerical strength."[72]
2. Kosmin and Lachman's recent study shows that UUs are sociologically above all religious groups.
   a. They calculated an aggregate score of four important social indicators: pattern of employment, extent of home ownership, level of education, and median family income.
   b. The Unitarian Universalists hold first place, followed by Disciples of Christ, agnostics, Congregationalists, and Episcopalians. (Jehovah's Witnesses are last, in thirtieth place.)[73]
3. Examples of UU Social Position
   a. Fully 49.5% of UUs are college graduates (with Jewish graduates at 46.7%, Roman Catholics at 20%, Mormons at 19.2%, and Baptists at 10.4%).[74]
   b. UU median annual household income is $34,800 (second only to Jewish respondents at $36,700).[75]
   c. UUs also have been disproportionately influential in U.S. institutions compared with other religious groups.[76]
      (1) Benjamin Rush, a signer of the Declaration of Independence[77]
      (2) Five U.S. presidents, namely, John Adams, John Quincy Adams, Thomas Jefferson,[78] Millard Fillmore, and William Howard Taft
      (3) Famous literary figures, including Henry Wadsworth Longfellow, Ralph Waldo Emerson, Herman Melville, e. e. cummings, William Cullen Bryant, Nathaniel Hawthorne, Horace Greeley, and Henry David Thoreau
      (4) Eight U.S. Supreme Court Justices, including Oliver Wendell Holmes
      (5) Architect Frank Lloyd Wright
      (6) Famous women, including Louisa May Alcott, Clara Barton, Julia Ward Howe, Florence Nightingale, and Susan B. Anthony

---

[72]Chandler, "Unitarians: Oneness in Diversity," 1.

[73]Kosmin and Lachman, 257, 262.

[74]Ibid., 258.

[75]Ibid., 260.

[76]Ibid., 252–53. Strictly speaking, before the1961 merger the individuals cited here would simply have been Unitarians, not Unitarian Universalists.

[77]Cassara, *Universalism in America,* 47, 89–94; Scholefield and Sawyer, "Our Roots," 7–8.

[78]Schulz, "About the Church of the Larger Fellowship," in *The Unitarian Universalist Pocket Guide,* 97; Russell Chandler, "Unitarians: Oneness in Diversity," *Los Angeles Times,* 27 May 1986, section I; Marshall, *Challenge of a Liberal Faith,* 29.

C. Publishers and Publications

1. Beacon Press

    a. Beacon Press is officially connected with the UUA and is the largest publisher of UU materials.

    b. Beacon also carries books by non-UU authors and on topics not directly linked to the UUA, particularily gay and lesbian concerns, Neo-pagan spirituality, and radical feminism.

    c. Beacon sells over half a million books annually.[79]

2. Skinner House Books

    a. Skinner House Books is officially connected to the UUA.

    b. Skinner's offerings tend to be more narrowly aimed at UUs.[80]

3. *World* Journal

    This bimonthly publication, with a circulation of over 115,000 households,[81] "includes features about UU values, purposes, aesthetics, spirituality, history, and personalities. It also carries news of UU individuals, congregations, and districts."[82]

4. *Connections*

    This is the bimonthly denominational newsletter.[83]

5. The Internet

    The UUA maintains a substantial presence on the Internet through their web page, links to other sites of interest to UUs, and a variety of online mailing lists.

D. Organizations Related to the UUA[84]

Below is a representative sampling of the organizations connected with the UUA. A complete listing is found in the UUA 1997–98 Directory.

1. Church of the Larger Fellowship (CLF)

    a. Founded in 1944, CLF serves geographically isolated religious liberals who have no access to a regular UU church.

    b. CLF is a "church without walls," serving its geographically separated members through "mail, phone, and fax,"[85] a lending library of UU resources, and a toll-free phone number to the "minister."

---

[79]Jack Mendelsohn, *Meet the Unitarian Universalists* (Boston: Unitarian Universalist Association, 1993), 16–17.

[80]Lawrence X. Peers, *The Congregational Handbook: How to Develop and Sustain Your Unitarian Universalist Congregation* (Boston: Unitarian Universalist Association, 1995), 15.

[81]*UUA 1997–98 Directory*, 25.

[82]Ibid.

[83]Peers, *Congregational Handbook*, 19.

[84]These are detailed in the *UUA 1997–98 Directory*, 397–436.

[85]Schulz, "About the Church of the Larger Fellowship," 96.

    c. CLF serves more than 2,200 members, including over 400 families, in sixty-five countries, all fifty of the United States, and all the Canadian provinces.[86]

    d. Scott W. Alexander is the minister of this "church" at this time.[87]

2. Associate Member Organizations of the UUA

    a. Unitarian Universalist Service Committee

      (1) "Founded in 1939 to help victims of fascism escape from Nazi-occupied Europe, the UUSC continues to promote social justice through public policy advocacy and support of local development initiatives."[88]

      (2) The UUSC boasts 20,000 members and supporters worldwide.

    b. Unitarian Universalist Women's Federation (UUWF)

      (1) The UUWF exists to advance a profeminist agenda and presents annual "Feminist Theology Awards."

      (2) "In 1994, the UUWF published 'Rise Up and Call Her Name,' a 13–session program exploring the multicultural roots of women's spirituality."[89]

3. Independent Affiliate Organizations

    a. Covenant of Unitarian Universalist Pagans (CUUPS)

    This group was founded at the 1985 General Assembly meeting for the purpose of promoting Neo-pagan, earth-centered spirituality within the UUA.[90]

    b. Friends of Religious Humanism (FRH)

    "Friends of Religious Humanism (FRH) was organized in 1963 to keep alive the religious element in humanism and the humanist element in liberal religion."[91]

    c. Interweave (Unitarian Universalists for Lesbian, Gay, Bisexual, and Transgender Concerns)

    "The organization is committed to work in areas of internalized homophobia, anti-racism, and ministry concerning lesbian, gay, bisexual, and transgender issues. There is also an annual sermon contest."[92]

    d. Unitarian Universalist Christian Fellowship (UUCF)

      (1) "The purposes of the Fellowship are to serve Christian [*sic*] Unitarians and Universalists according to their expressed reli-

---

[86]Ibid.

[87]*UUA 1997–98 Directory*, 63.

[88]*UUA 1995–96 Directory*, 350.

[89]*UUA 1997–98 Directory*, 399.

[90]Ibid., 402.

[91]Ibid., 403.

[92]Ibid., 404.

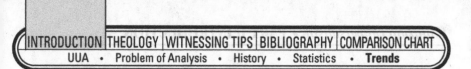
gious needs; to uphold and promote the Christian witness within the UUA; and to uphold and promote the historic Unitarian and Universalist witness and conscience within the church universal."[93]

(2) The UUCF publishes a bimonthly newsletter (*Good News*) and a quarterly journal (*The Unitarian Universalist Christian*).[94]

E. Educational Institutions

Below are a few of the more popular schools where UUA ministers receive their theological training:

1. Harvard Divinity School
2. Meadville/Lombard Theological School (affiliated with the University of Chicago Divinity School)
3. Starr King School for the Ministry

V. Current Trends in the UUA

A. "Evangelism" in the UUA

1. Unlike the past, UUs are now actively seeking converts.

   a. For most of its history, the UUA eschewed "evangelism" or seeking converts. Evangelism by nature was seen as inimical to the twin ideals of tolerance and pluralism.[95]

   b. However, systematic efforts at outreach and growth have now become fashionable among newer and more aggressive UUs.[96]

   c. Neil Chethik observes, "UUA officials have even begun using . . . 'the dreaded e-word.' The association's new training course, *Sharing the Unitarian Universalist Faith,* includes 'evangelism' in its subtitle."[97]

   d. Former UUA president William F. Schulz has vowed to make Unitarian Universalism "a household word."[98]

   e. Scott Alexander's book *Salted with Fire* presents a militant program of expansion through evangelism.[99]

---

[93]Ibid., 406.

[94]Ibid. A circulation figure of 1,200 was given to me in a phone call (31 July 1995) with Dr. Thomas Wintle.

[95]Marshall, "Unitarian Universalism," 300. See also Marshall, *Challenge of a Liberal Faith,* 237.

[96]Tony Larsen, "Evangelizing Our Children," in *Salted with Fire: Unitarian Universalist Strategies for Sharing Faith and Growing Congregations,* ed. Scott W. Alexander (Boston: Skinner House, 1995), 124.

[97]Neil Chethik, "The Saving Message: The New UU Evangelists," *The World* 9, no. 3 (May/June 1995): 18. On the traditional reluctance of UUs even to use the word "evangelism" in polite company, see also Alexander, "Introduction," in *Salted with Fire,* 1.

[98]Chandler, "Unitarians: Oneness in Diversity," 1, 20.

[99]For a biographical sketch of Alexander, see Craig Wilson, "Minister Preaches Gay Acceptance," *USA Today,* 20 August 1991, sec. D, p. 4.

2. Fueling this new interest in outreach is a desire to counteract the so-called Religious Right.[100]

   Alexander states, "The religious right has shown us how endangered our values are, how high are the stakes. We're realizing that if we don't stand up in the public square and proclaim our beliefs, our message will never be heard."[101]

3. UUs are using "church growth" strategies, often borrowed from growing evangelical denominations.

   a. "Religious liberals can learn from and employ these evangelical methods," Alexander stated, "without in any way adopting, mimicking, or supporting their orthodox message."[102]

   b. The growth-oriented UUs are courting the baby boomers,[103] and a *Newsweek* article dubbed the UUA the "quintessential boomer church."[104]

B. *"Spirituality" in the UUA*

1. The Decline of Humanism and the Increase in "Spiritual" Interest Among UUs

   a. Humanists Kurtz and Bullough lament, "While humanism is influential in the UUA, it is not the dominant voice.... humanism seems to be diminishing in influence as a spiritualistic concern begins to be felt more strongly."[105]

   b. Gustav Neibuhr points out that many UUA pulpits have abandoned their "cool, cerebral sermons on the greatness of human reason" and now preach a more "spiritual" message instead.[106]

   c. While it is still true that "intellectual stimulation" remains an important part of UU worship, it is also true, as Arvid Straube notes, that "[the baby boomer seekers in UU churches] are thirsty for spirit from whatever source."[107]

---

[100]For example, note the resolution passed at the 1996 UUA General Assembly entitled "Challenging the Radical Right" (see their web site, http://www.uua.org). See also Larry B. Stammer, "6 Churches Seek to Foil Religious Right Agenda," *Los Angeles Times*, 9 December 1995, Home Edition, Metro section; Elyce Wakerman, "Groups Aim to Reverse Gains of Religious Right," *Los Angeles Times*, 18 November 1995, Home Edition, Metro section; and Elyce Wakerman, "Alliance Seeks to Counter Religious Right," *Los Angeles Times*, 29 June 1996, Home Edition, Metro section.

[101]Chethik, "The Saving Message," 14.

[102]Alexander, "Introduction," in *Salted with Fire*, 2.

[103]Meyer, "Courting the Baby Boomers," in *Salted with Fire*, 94. On the eclectic spiritual tastes of the baby boom and generation X'ers, see also Mary Rourke, "Build-It-Yourself Religion," *Los Angeles Times*, 17 June 1996, Home Edition, Life and Style section.

[104]See Kenneth L. Woodward et al., "And the Children Shall Lead Them: Young Americans Return to God," *Newsweek*, 17 December 1990, 50–56.

[105]Kurtz and Bullough, "The Unitarian Universalist Association: Humanism or Theism?" 13–14.

[106]Gustav Neibuhr, "With a New Spiritualism, Unitarians Welcome People of All Beliefs," *Washington Post*, 6 July 1993, A3.

[107]Straube, "Spirituality and Church Growth," in *Salted with Fire*, 173; UUA, *The Quality of Religious Life in UU Congregations*, 5.

2. New Age

    a. For some UUs, New Age spirituality seems to fit the bill.

    b. The UUA's seventh principle in its *Statement of Principles and Purposes* embodies a New Age emphasis when it speaks of the UUA's "respect for the interdependent web of all existence."[108]

    c. For example, UU Ann Fields speaks of "our collective consciousness which, in every instant of time, grows richer and more vibrant, as the universe becomes aware of itself." This process she calls God, "the spiritual evolution of the cosmos—creation flowing free."[109]

    d. Past president Schulz cites approvingly New Ager Fritjof Capra's monistic worldview, embracing a "deep ecology" of the "divine One."[110]

3. Neo-paganism[111] and Radical Feminism

    a. Neo-pagans have also made significant inroads in the UUA.

    Schulz affirms that paganism "fits very neatly with our tradition. . . . For us, a religion grounded in nature is part and parcel of our heritage."[112]

    b. The Covenant of Unitarian Universalist Pagans (CUUPS), formed in 1985, is the main official affiliate group for Neo-pagan UUs, with sixty chapters nationwide.[113]

    c. Some of the interest in Neo-paganism, though not all, is connected to radical feminism.

        (1) Kosmin and Lachman observe that goddess religions have become increasingly important in some feminist circles.[114]

        (2) The UUA has warmly embraced this feminist Neo-pagan fringe.

        (3) For example, there is a "popular Unitarian course" entitled "Cakes for the Queen of Heaven," which teaches women about worshiping the goddess.[115]

---

[108]The UUA adopted the *Principles and Purposes* as bylaws at the 1984 and 1985 General Assemblies. They are reproduced in numerous UUA publications. See, for example, the *UUA 1997–98 Directory*, 3.

[109]Fields, "Continuous Creation," in *Unitarian Universalist Views of God,* ed. Doris Hunter (Boston: Unitarian Universalist Association, n.d.), 3.

[110]Chandler, "Unitarians: Oneness in Diversity," 21.

[111]For a thorough treatment of Neo-pagan beliefs and practices, see Craig S. Hawkins, *Goddess Worship, Witchcraft and Neo-Paganism* (Grand Rapids: Zondervan, 1998), in this series; see also his book *Witchcraft: Exploring the World of Wicca* (Grand Rapids: Baker, 1996).

[112]Kosmin and Lachman, *One Nation Under God,* 154, citing Schulz.

[113]Don Lattin, "Pagans to Light Up the Year's Longest Night," *San Francisco Chronicle,* 21 December 1991, section A, p. 19. See also IV.D.3.a above.

[114]Some scholars, however, present convincing evidence that most of these historic religions were not actually matriarchal or goddess dominated at all. For example, see Tikva Frymer-Kensky, *In the Wake of the Goddesses: Women, Culture and the Biblical Transformation of Pagan Myth* (New York: Fawcett Columbine, 1992).

[115]Christina Robb, "In Goddesses They Trust," *Boston Globe,* 9 July 1990, sec. 32. The article also mentions that goddess religion is a "hot" topic at some theology schools, such as Episcopal and Harvard Divinity in Cambridge. This is due to the emphasis on women's issues in those schools.

   d. Current UUA hymnody reflects Neo-pagan influences.

     (1) The revised hymnbook, *Singing the Living Tradition*,[116] contains Neo-pagan hymns.

     (2) This hymnal includes hymns and readings such as the song "We are Dancing Sarah's Circle" by feminist theologian Nelle Morton; a reading entitled "The Womb of the Stars" by Joy Atkinson ("written to acknowledge and celebrate the 'interdependent web' of existence, using maternal imagery to speak about the cosmos-source of our being"); a reading entitled "I who am the beauty of the green earth" from Starhawk's *Spiral Dance;* and Starhawk's prayer entitled "Earth Mother, Star Mother."[117]

C. Social Activism in the UUA

The UUA is well known for its social activism and typically aligns itself with politically liberal social causes. Below are a few of the more prominent issues of concern to UUs.

1. Gay and Lesbian Rights

   a. The UUA was one of the first denominations to ordain gays and lesbians to the ministry (1970).

     In a brochure entitled "Unitarian Universalism: A Religious Home for Gay, Lesbian, and Bisexual People," Barbara Pescan notes, "Compared to other denominations, we have by far the highest percentage of ... openly gay and lesbian clergy."[118]

   b. "Since 1970, the Unitarian Universalist Association (UUA) has enacted a total of 10 resolutions in support of lesbian, gay, and bisexual persons and their particular needs."[119]

   c. In 1984 the UUA General Assembly became the first denomination to perform "services of union" between gay couples.[120]

   d. Following the "mandate" of its General Assembly, in 1989 the UUA launched its Welcoming Congregation Program in outreach to gays, lesbians, and bisexuals.[121]

   e. In 1996 the UUA voted to endorse legalizing same-sex marriages, "making it the first denomination in the country to do so." By a

---

[116]Unitarian Universalist Association, *Singing the Living Tradition* (Boston: Beacon, 1993).

[117]Jacqui James, ed., *Between the Lines: Sources for Singing the Living Tradition* (Boston: Unitarian Universalist Association, 1995), 59, 103, 116–117.

[118]Barbara Pescan, *Unitarian Universalism: A Religious Home for Gay, Lesbian, and Bisexual People* (Boston: Unitarian Universalist Association, n.d.). Note that while 90% of UUs surveyed believe that homosexuality is an acceptable lifestyle, two-thirds also reported that homosexuality would factor negatively in their decision to hire a minister. See UUA, *The Quality of Religious Life in UU Congregations*, 16.

[119] Ibid.

[120]Ibid.; see also Schulz, "Foreword," in *Our Chosen Faith*, xiii.

[121]Peers, *Congregational Handbook*, 202–3.

vote of 667 to 19, the UUs proclaimed "the worth of marriage between any two committed persons."[122]

2. Abortion Rights

   a. The UUA takes a decidedly pro-abortion stance.

   b. Rev. Steve Edington stated, "As an institution, we are strongly pro-choice, as are most individual UUs."[123]

   c. The UUA 1996 General Assembly advocated "the right of every woman to safe, effective, and affordable abortion services."[124] It is further stated that "congregations and individual Unitarian Universalists be encouraged to establish and support specific projects in their communities to help implement these goals."

3. Doctor-assisted Suicide

   a. "The denomination endorsed such actions as part of a right-to-death-with-dignity resolution it adopted in 1988."[125]

   b. The UUs have supported various ballot initiatives, such as those in Washington state and Oregon, to legalize euthanasia for the terminally ill.[126]

4. Feminism

   a. When compared with other denominations, the UUA boasts the highest percentage of female clergy (25%).[127] "Including those in training, almost half the ministers in the Unitarian Universalist Association are women."[128]

   b. The UUA has excised "sexist and patriarchal language from its statement of faith."[129]

---

[122]The text of the resolution is entitled "Support of the Right to Marry for Same-Sex Couples," and can be found on the UUA Internet site (http://www.uua.org). See also "Unitarians Endorse Same-Sex Marriages," B-5.

[123]Sias, *100 Questions,* 39.

[124]Resolution entitled "Population and Development," 1996 UUA General Assembly (text available at http://www.uua.org).

[125]See "Religion Briefs; Bishops Oppose Legal Euthanasia," *Los Angeles Times,* 14 September 1991, Home Edition, Calendar section, p. F-17.

[126]John Balzar, "Washington State Voters May Grant the Right to Die; Medicine: Pioneering Ballot Measure Could Make Doctor-Assisted Suicide a Legal Option for Terminally Ill," *Los Angeles Times,* 6 October 1991, Home Edition, A-1; Associated Press, "Measure on Suicide Fought by Churches; Election: Catholic Sources Give Most of the $1 Million That Finances the Campaign Against Oregon Proposal. It Would Allow Doctors to Prescribe Lethal Drugs to Terminally Ill," *Los Angeles Times,* 5 November 1994, Home Edition, Metro section, B-4.

[127]Pescan, *"Unitarian Universalism: A Religious Home for Gay, Lesbian, and Bisexual People."*

[128]Sias, *100 Questions,* 25. See also UUA, *The Quality of Religious Life in UU Congregations,* 17, which presents even higher numbers.

[129]Kosmin and Lachman, *One Nation Under God,* 228. See also Judith Meyer, *The Faith of a Feminist* (Boston: Unitarian Universalist Association, 1994), on the 1977 UUA General Assembly resolution.

Part II:
Theology

I. Religious Freedom, Tolerance, and Pluralism

A. *The Unitarian Universalist Position on Religious Freedom, Pluralism, and Tolerance Briefly Stated*[1]

1. People should be free to choose and to craft their own religious beliefs.
2. Freedom of belief is incompatible with subscription to creeds or statements of faith.
3. UUs promote religious tolerance and pluralism as a virtue. Conversely, UUs eschew religious exclusivism.
4. UUs do in fact put their pluralistic ideals into practice. One finds a wide variety of "faith stances" in the UUA.
5. Nevertheless, UUs are *not* free to believe absolutely anything they want or to believe in nothing at all.[2]
6. Some UUs draw on the Christian tradition while others do not. In any case, UUs do not view Christianity as exclusively true.
7. The Christian faith, rightly understood, is compatible with being a UU.

B. *Arguments Used by Unitarian Universalists to Support Their View of Religious Freedom, Pluralism, and Tolerance*

1. People should be free to choose and to craft their own religious beliefs.

    a. "The Unitarian Universalist church is nonmissionary. We believe that every person has a right to his or her own religious position so long as it does not trespass upon the rights of others."[3]

    b. "There will be one unifying principle [among UUs]: namely, the right to make up one's own mind about what one believes."[4]

    c. "Unitarian Universalists believe that all persons must decide about God for themselves."[5]

2. Freedom of belief is incompatible with subscription to creeds or statements of faith.

    a. UUs are not "required to accept a dogmatic creed."[6]

---

[1]To establish the UU position in each of the "A" and "B" points of the theology section, I have relied exclusively on Unitarian Universalist authors.

[2]This point may seem to run counter to the one above, but it is the UU position. See I.B.5 below.

[3]George N. Marshall, *Challenge of a Liberal Faith*, rev. and enl. (New Canaan, Conn.: Keats, 1980), 237.

[4]Jack Mendelsohn, *Meet the Unitarian Universalists* (Boston: Unitarian Universalist Association, 1993), 2.

[5]Karl M. Chworowsky and Christopher Gist Raible, "What Is a Unitarian Universalist?" in *Religions in America,* ed. Leo Rosten (New York: Simon and Schuster, 1975), 265.

[6]Ibid., 264.

b. "Ours is a non-creedal, non-doctrinal religion which affirms the individual's freedom of belief."[7]

c. "Unitarianism, then, has meant first of all religious freedom and escape from bondage to creeds; and throughout their whole history Unitarians have steadfastly refused to set up any creed, even the shortest, as a test which must be passed by those who would join them."[8]

d. The *Principles and Purposes* of the UUA, adopted as bylaws at the 1984 and 1985 General Assemblies, is the closest UUs come to a creed or statement of faith.

(1) All UUA congregations give assent to this document.

(2) However, this statement deals only in broad strokes, affirming primarily such values as "tolerance," "freedom of thought," "justice," and "the inherent worth of human beings."

3. UUs promote religious tolerance and pluralism as a virtue. Conversely, UUs eschew religious exclusivism.

a. "Another major Unitarian affirmation is a belief in universality, which excludes all exclusiveness."[9]

b. Because truth is not absolute but relative and changing, UUs tolerate a wide variety of religious perspectives.[10]

(1) "All people should be tolerant of the religious ideas of others. Truth is not absolute; it changes over time."[11]

(2) UU James Luther Adams states, "It [Unitarianism] protests against the idolatry of any human claim to absolute truth or authority."[12]

c. Because truth is found in many sources, UUs believe that tolerance and pluralism are virtuous.

(1) "Unitarian Universalists believe that no religion—including their own—has exclusive possession of the truth. All ought to be honored and respected for the truths in them. The following of almost any religion can help a dedicated individual find a better and more meaningful life."[13]

---

[7]Sias, *100 Questions That Non-Members Ask About Unitarian Universalism* (n.p.: Transition Publishing, 1994), 7.

[8]Wilbur, *Our Unitarian Heritage,* 468.

[9]Phillip Hewett, *The Unitarian Way* (Toronto: Canadian Unitarian Council, 1985), 89.

[10]See William F. Schulz, "Set on a Mission [Finding Time: Reflections from the President of the UUA]," *The World* 5, no. 6 (November/December 1991): 2; and F. Forrester Church, "The Cathedral of the World," in *Our Chosen Faith: An Introduction to Unitarian Universalism* (Boston: Beacon, 1989), 96.

[11]Sias, *100 Questions,* 1.

[12]James Luther Adams, "The Church as Liberator," in *Unitarian Universalist Views of Church,* ed. Lawrence X. Peers (Boston: Unitarian Universalist Association, 1992).

[13]Chworowsky and Raible, "What Is a Unitarian Universalist?" 272.

(2) "No one person, no one faith, no one book, no one institution has all the answers, nor even any patent on the way of finding answers."[14]

4. UUs do in fact practice pluralism. One finds a wide variety of "faith stances" in the UUA.[15]

   a. "Found in today's [UU] churches are humanism, agnosticism, atheism, theism, liberal Christianity, neo-paganism and earth spiritualism. These beliefs are not mutually exclusive—it's possible to hold more than one."[16]

   b. The following is a classification of faith stances found in the UUA:[17]

      (1) Liberal Christian theism—UUs who regard themselves as "Christians," with a "Christianity" of a liberal, not orthodox,[18] variety

      (2) Non-Christian theism[19]—Some oriented toward a particular non-Christian religion, such as UU Judaism, and others toward a syncretistic blend of various options

      (3) Pantheistic belief systems[20]—New Age,[21] Neo-paganism and goddess worship;[22] and other forms of earth-centered spirituality

      (4) Nontheistic (atheistic) humanism

5. Nevertheless, UUs are *not* free to believe absolutely anything they want or to believe in nothing at all.

   a. "Unitarian Universalism is not the *freedom* to believe anything or nothing."[23]

   b. "It is *not* true that one can subscribe to views at variance with our most basic values. Clearly, one could never advocate racism or

---

[14]Hewett, *The Unitarian Way,* 89.

[15]See, for example, the Unitarian Universalist Association, *The Quality of Religious Life in Unitarian Universalist Congregations: A Survey by the Commission on Appraisal* (Boston: Unitarian Universalist Association, 1989), 31, 46–47.

[16]Sias, *100 Questions,* 2. See also Tom Owen-Towle, *Welcome to Unitarian Universalism: A Community of Truth, Service, Holiness and Love* (Boston: Unitarian Universalist Association, n.d.).

[17]My summary is a modification of Hoehler's classification of faith stances within the UUA. (Hoehler is a UU "Christian.") See Harry H. Hoehler, "Is There a Place for UU Christians in the UUA? A Reply and Some Reflections," *Unitarian Universalist Christian* 38, nos. 3–4 (Fall/Winter 1983): 6–7.

[18]In this book I use the word "orthodox" in its most general sense of "correct teaching." I am not referring to the tradition of Eastern Orthodoxy.

[19]"Theism is the view that all limited or finite things are dependent in some way on one supreme or ultimate reality of which one may also speak in personal terms" (*Encyclopedia Britannica,* on-line edition [http://www.eb.com], s.v. "theism").

[20]Pantheism is the belief that God is all and all is God. Pantheists deny that God is personal.

[21]On New Age pantheism, see Ron Rhodes, *New Age Movement* (Grand Rapids: Zondervan, 1995), 46–49, in this series.

[22]As Craig Hawkins points out, one finds a wide range of views of God among Neo-pagans, a major one of which is pantheism. See Craig S. Hawkins, *Goddess Worship, Witchcraft and Neo-Paganism* (Grand Rapids: Zondervan, 1998), in this series.

[23]Elizabeth May Strong, *Can I Believe Anything I Want?* (Boston: Unitarian Universalist Association, 1994).

genocide, for example, and still in any meaningful sense call one-self a Unitarian Universalist."[24]

   c. "It is nonsense for critics to say that one can believe whatever one-likes and still be a Unitarian. It is not possible to believe in the virtues of racism, totalitarianism, irrationalism and dogmatism and still be a Unitarian."[25]

   d. "You don't get to believe just anything you want to in Unitarian Universalism. Belief in the KKK or the Nazis or bigotry—and a host of other things—are not tolerated here. So people don't get to believe just anything they want to here, and we also stand for much more than freedom of belief, as important as that is."[26]

6. Some UUs draw on the Christian tradition while others do not. In any case, UUs do not view Christianity as exclusively true.

   a. Some UUs consider themselves "liberal Christians."

      (1) Though in the minority (i.e., between 10 and 20%), nonethe-less, as President John A. Buehrens states, Unitarian Univer-salist Christians have "an honored place in our midst."[27]

      (2) The Unitarian Universalist Christian Fellowship is the main support organization for Christians in the UUA.[28]

   b. Most Unitarian Universalists regard themselves simply as "reli-gious liberals," though not as Christians.

      (1) Duke Gray observes, "The vast majority of congregations now belonging to the UUA consider themselves non-Christian."[29]

      (2) Most UUs are some flavor of humanist, with some turning to Neo-paganism and other alternative forms of spirituality.

   c. Some non-Christian UUs draw on aspects of the Christian tradition together with other religious traditions.

      (1) Diane Winston notes, "It is more likely for church members to say Christianity is one of many traditions they draw upon."[30]

      (2) The official UU hymnbook, *Singing the Living Tradition*, con-tains many Christian hymns and readings.[31]

---

[24]William F. Schulz, "Our Faith," in *The Unitarian Universalist Pocket Guide*, 4.

[25]Hewett, *The Unitarian Way*, 82.

[26]Tony A. Larsen, "Evangelizing Our Children," in *Salted with Fire*, 127. See also William F. Schulz, "Theology According to *Newsweek* [Finding Time: Reflections from the President of the UUA]," *The World* (May/June 1991): 2.

[27]Chandler, "Unitarians: Oneness in Diversity," 1, 21. A 1989 survey places the number at 19 percent. See UUA, *The Quality of Religious Life in UU Congregations*, 31–32, 46.

[28]*Unitarian Universalist Association 1997–98 Directory* (Boston: Unitarian Universalist Association, 1995), 406.

[29]Duke T. Gray, "Letter to the Christians," *Unitarian Universalist Christian* 47, nos. 3–4 (Fall/Winter 1992): 42.

[30]Diane Winston, "Unitarian 'Boomer' Following Growing," *Denver Post*, 9 May 1991, 2A.

[31]UUs have adjusted the wording of many hymns to fit Unitarian theological and political sensibilities. For example, in Luther's "A Mighty Fortress" one finds a verse altered to read, "Man is the earth upright and

    d. Other non-Christian UUs do not draw on aspects of Christianity but would claim that their faith stance draws primarily from an altogether different religious tradition.

7. The Christian faith, rightly understood, is compatible with being a UU.

    a. Tony Larsen objects to those who say that one cannot be both a UU and a Christian: "And yet, I often hear Unitarian Universalists say, 'Oh, I'm not a Christian—I'm a Unitarian Universalist.' Folks, that is a misleading thing to say. . . . phrasing your answer that way is bound to give people the impression that being a Christian and being Unitarian Universalist are incompatible. And that they most certainly are not!"[32]

    b. Larsen continues, "If any of the things Jesus taught speak to your life, and hint at what it means to live a truly human life, then I'd say you're free to call yourself a Christian—if you wish to use any labels at all."[33]

    c. The UUA's "Statement of Principles and Purposes" explicitly identifies certain Christian teachings as part of the "living tradition."

C. Refutation of Arguments Used by Unitarian Universalists to Support Their View of Religious Freedom, Pluralism, and Tolerance

1. UUs confuse their *right* to believe with the expectation that others must respect the *validity* and *correctness* of UU beliefs.

    a. UUs proclaim their "freedom of belief" and the "right" to believe what they want. Yet in the United States (where virtually all UUs reside) it is not clear that anyone denies them the "right" to be UUs or to believe whatever they want, however logically and theologically indefensible.

    b. Though UUs have a right to believe whatever they want, it does not follow that they have a "right" to demand that non-UUs embrace their beliefs or even take these beliefs seriously—especially since Unitarian Universalism is fraught with difficulties.

    c. Christians agree that "all persons must decide about God for themselves." Because saving faith cannot be legislated or imposed by force, evangelical Christians emphasize the need for personal faith in Christ (John 1:12). Yet this is entirely compatible with Christians seeking to help others achieve responsible, intellectually sound, spiritually healthy beliefs, based on sound reasons (2 Tim. 2:24–26).

2. The UU attack against exclusivistic religious beliefs is self-refuting, contradictory, and illogical.

---

proud" (see Robert B. Tapp, "The Unitarian Universalists: Style and Substance," *Christian Century* 96, no. 9 [1979]: 277). Similarly, the hymn "For All the Saints" removes references to Jesus.

[32]Tony Larsen with Ellen Schmidt, *A Catechism for Unitarian Universalists (Leader Guide)* (Boston: Unitarian Universalist Association, 1989), 8.

[33]Ibid., 9.

a. Phillip Hewett's statement that UU pluralism "excludes all exclusiveness" highlights well the self-refuting nature of the UU position.

b. It is impossible for UUs to exclude all exclusivistic positions since the very act of excluding these positions is itself an act of exclusivism. This act, in turn, would have to be excluded, which is yet another act of exclusivism needing exclusion, and so on.

c. UUs themselves admit that one cannot believe whatever one wants and be a UU.[34] That is to say, some propositions are seen as incompatible with the tenets of Unitarian Universalism.[35] This demonstrates that UUs are indeed "intolerant" toward some positions (e.g., Nazism, the KKK).

d. Like all belief systems, Unitarian Universalism excludes certain beliefs even as it affirms others. The issue, then, is not *whether* some beliefs will be excluded but only *which ones* and *why*.

e. It is therefore fair to ask on what basis beliefs are excluded or accepted.

   (1) For example, both Christians and UUs denounce racism and the KKK. The difference is that Christians have an objective, biblical basis (Gal. 3:28) for doing so while UUs have no objective basis, given their relativistic view of truth.[36]

   (2) Since UUs remove any objective moral basis for excluding the KKK, the most a UU can say is that he or she personally finds the KKK reprehensible, not that it is wrong objectively. By contrast, biblical Christians say racism is always wrong, no matter how an individual or even an entire society feels about it.

   (3) If "truth is not absolute" and "changes over time," there is no basis for denying the possibility that UUs might consider racism virtuous tomorrow even though they do not do so today.

f. The UU attack against "religious exclusivism" on the basis that "truth is not absolute" and "changes over time" is logically absurd.

   (1) The statement "truth is not absolute" is offered as being absolutely true. The statement refutes itself.

   (2) If we should not make exclusivistic claims because "truth changes over time," then what if one of the "truths" that "changes over time" turns out to be the "truth" that "truth changes over time"? Or the "truth" that exclusivism is bad and pluralism is good? Are UUs willing to allow that tomorrow's UU "truth" might be that pluralism is no longer good? In being unwilling to admit any of these things, they tacitly affirm the

---

[34]See I.B.5 above.
[35]The *Statement of Principles and Purposes* is discussed at I.B.2.d above.
[36]See I.B.3.b above.

goodness of pluralism as a timeless truth, in spite of the fact that they deny the existence of timeless truth.

3. Exclusive truth claims do not necessarily entail arrogance or lack of humility.

   a. It is not arrogant to claim that $2 + 2 = 4$ and *only* 4, even though the claim excludes other answers as correct.

   b. If it is arrogant to believe that one is right and others wrong, then UUs are arrogant since they believe that they are right and Christian "fundamentalists" are wrong.

   c. Consider the Christian belief that Jesus Christ is God's *only* provision for salvation.

      (1) Jesus himself taught this (John 10:1, 7; 14:6). So when Christians affirm the same thing, they are "guilty" merely of believing that Jesus told the truth, not of being arrogant.

      (2) Now Jesus' claim is either true or false. If it is true, then Christians are simply telling the truth when they affirm Jesus' claim. If Jesus' claim is false, then Christians are "guilty" only of having been duped. Arrogance has nothing to do with it.

      (3) Furthermore, if it is *rational* to believe it to be true, then one *ought* to believe it and seek to persuade others of its truth.

   c. Note that when the UUs urge "Exclusivistic statements are arrogant," they themselves are making an arrogant statement (on UU terms), because such a statement is itself exclusivistic: It excludes those who disagree with it (e.g., evangelical Christians).

   d. In dogmatically rejecting the Christian claim of salvation in Jesus alone without even allowing that it *might* be true, they are hardly "open to *every* revelation"![37]

4. Many UUs are actually intolerant of the liberal UU "Christians."

   a. In some writings of prominent UU "Christians," it is apparent that UU tolerance toward even them is surprisingly lacking.

   b. Statements by UU "Christians" themselves belie president Buehrens's claim that they have an "honored place" in the UUA.[38]

      (1) In 1976 prominent UU "Christian" Harry H. Hoehler lamented, "We recognize that it has been increasingly difficult for Christians to continue to stay within Unitarian Universalism.... The cause of our discomfort is the dominance of naturalistic humanism as a new orthodoxy in the Association. It is a new Pharisaism."[39]

---

[37]Schulz, "Set on a Mission," 2.

[38]The following quotes come from the official UUA journal, *The Unitarian Universalist Christian*. The conclusions are based, at least in part, on hard statistical data.

[39]Unitarian Universalist Christian Fellowship (UUCF) Task Force, "Memoranda and Documents: Report of the UUCF Task Force on Mission (1976)," *Unitarian Universalist Christian* 47, nos. 3–4 (Fall/Winter 1992): 67.

(2) Seven years later, commenting on the results of a question-naire surveying UU attitudes, Hoehler said, ". . . a significant number of the comments returned were decidedly anti-Christian in both tone and content. Granted, such sentiment is hardly new. What the questionnaire did was highlight how extensive it is."[40]

(3) Other UUs have made similar observations more recently.[41]

5. Some faith stances in the UUA are mutually exclusive and contradictory.

a. Steve Edington and others affirm a patent contradiction when they say that the different faith stances in the UUA "are not mutually exclusive" and that "it's possible to hold more than one."[42]

(1) Edington cites atheism and theism as examples of different faith stances in the UUA that are not mutually exclusive. But atheism is the view that there is no God, whereas theism is the view that there is a God. One cannot affirm a contradiction without being irrational.

(2) Perhaps because of UU pluralism, the UU tent is big enough to accept people with irrational beliefs. However, as noted earlier, irrationalism is one of the views that Hewett *excludes* from Unitarian Universalism.[43]

(3) Some of the faith stances in the UUA explicitly and self-consciously *celebrate* irrationality. Neo-paganism is but one example of this.[44] Therefore, Neo-pagan UUs ought to be offended at Hewett's intolerant, exclusivistic statements.

b. Even some UUs acknowledge the inability of these different faith stances to coexist logically.

Duke Gray states, "We represent a plural list of religious options—many of them contradictory. This new pluralism brought an end to any pretense that a common faith binds us. We are no longer a religion. We are an Association of religions."[45]

6. The UU attack against "creeds" is fraught with difficulties.

a. UUs wrongly assume that if one affirms a "creed" that this necessarily short-circuits critical thinking and freedom of belief.

b. A creed (from the Latin *credere*, "to believe") is nothing more than a statement of belief. While creeds may vary in detail, complexity, and length, they are nothing more than affirmations of belief.

---

[40]Hoehler, "Is There a Place for UU Christians in the UUA?" 16.

[41]For example, see Gray's 1992 "Letter to the Christians," 49–50.

[42]Sias, *100 Questions*, 2.

[43]See I.B.5.c above.

[44]Hawkins demonstrates this in *Goddess Worship, Witchcraft and Neo-paganism*; see also Craig S. Hawkins, *Witchcraft: Exploring the World of Wicca* (Grand Rapids: Baker, 1996), 161.

[45]Gray, "Letter to the Christians," 41; see also 42, 44, and comments on the Bylaws on 49.

    c. The UUs have "creeds"—statements articulating their beliefs.

        (1) UUs often make statements such as "Unitarian Universalists do not believe in creeds" or "Creeds are bad," and such utterances are offered as statements of core UU belief. How such statements differ from creeds is difficult to see.

        (2) As noted earlier, the UUA *Principles and Purposes* statement sets forth UU beliefs and values.

        (3) Resolutions at the UUA General Assembly sometimes include "confessions" of UU convictions (e.g., belief in same-sex marriages, the moral right of women to choose abortion).

    d. The UUs may object that their statements are not "creeds" because they are not "binding." However, as already shown, UUs cannot deny their "most basic values" and remain UUs. The UUA has enunciated these core principles in many places (e.g., the *Principles and Purposes* statement), and belief in them is not optional for UUs.

    e. The UU may also object that their statements of belief deal only with "principles" rather than with the specifics of belief. However, his would prove only that UUs have a less detailed or vague creed.[46] And these principles do relate to specific behaviors and beliefs. For example, UUs would undoubtedly ban a Grand Wizard of the KKK for his racism (a specific behavior) based on their general principle of "the inherent worth and dignity of every person."

    f. UUs assume that orthodox (i.e., biblical) Christians do not think for themselves if they affirm a creed. However, it is arrogant to assume automatically that Christians do not intellectually evaluate the truth of their belief system.

  7. True, biblical Christians are "inclusive" even though they are not pluralistic about the way in which one must be saved.

    This is discussed more fully at point D.4 below.

    a. Contrary to UU assertions, theologically conservative Christians are not narrow and divisive but are actually "inclusive" in the sense that they want all people to join them as part of God's family.

    b. If Jesus really is the only way of salvation, as he himself claimed and as Christians believe, then it would be heartless and uncompassionate for Christians either to remain silent or to acknowledge different (and therefore false) paths to salvation.

    c. At most the UU could charge the Christian with being deluded or otherwise mistaken but not with being exclusivistic (in their pejorative understanding of the word) or divisive. Indeed, if Christians

---

[46]On this point see Hoehler, "Is There a Place for UU Christians in the UUA?" 8–9.

genuinely *were* exclusivistic, they would ignore UUs and other unbelievers, but they desire *all* to be saved (1 Tim. 2:4).

8. The form of "Christianity" embraced by those UUs who claim to be Christian is counterfeit and cultic.

    a. The Christian faith has certain defining characteristics, which make it Christian and not something else. (See point D.5.)

    b. *All* religions (including Unitarian Universalism) have certain core teachings that define them; Christianity is no exception.

    c. Contrary to Tony Larsen's assertion, one is not a Christian simply because some saying or other of Jesus might prove inspirational.

        (1) To be a Christian, one must believe in the central doctrines of Christianity, just as to be a Unitarian Universalist one must believe in their core principles.

        (2) Just as "it is nonsense for critics to say that one can believe whatever one likes and still be a Unitarian,"[47] even so, it is nonsense for Larsen to say that a person can disbelieve the core doctrines of Christianity and still call oneself a Christian.

    d. Because UUs deny the central doctrines of the Christian faith, any Christian allegiance they may claim is counterfeit and thus cultic.[48]

D. The Biblical View of Religious Freedom, Pluralism, and Tolerance

1. God does not tolerate pluralism in religious belief.

    a. Even though non-Christian religions may contain certain elements of truth, they are fundamentally false.

        (1) Some non-Christian religions affirm, among other things, that God exists and that there is only one true God,[49] but these systems are fundamentally corrupt in that they do not lead a person toward, but away from, the true God of the Bible.

        (2) Paul acknowledged that the Athenians' religion had elements of truth (e.g., Acts 17:28), but nonetheless declared that they worshiped ignorantly (v. 23) and idolatrously (v. 29).

    b. We see in the Old Testament that God's judgment fell on nations for their idolatrous worship (Deut. 18:9–12). Yahweh denounced and threatened those who followed after other gods (Deut. 13) and demanded that the Israelites worship him and him alone (Ex. 20:3).

    c. Likewise, the New Testament condemnation of religious pluralism is entirely consistent with that of the Old.

        (1) Paul says that those who worshiped created things (e.g., as Neo-pagans do today) "exchanged the truth of God for a lie"

---

[47]Hewett, *The Unitarian Way*, 82.

[48]For a definition of a "cult," see Alan W. Gomes, *Unmasking the Cults* (Grand Rapids: Zondervan, 1995), 7–12, in this series.

[49]The "one God," however, is not Triune and does not possess the nature and attributes ascribed to God in Scripture.

(Rom. 1:25). For this reason "God gave them over to shameful lusts" (1:26). This hardly shows "tolerance" on God's part.

    (2) Jesus Christ alone is declared to be God's way of salvation (see IV.C.4 and VI.D.2 below).

d. That only Christians will be in heaven (see VII.C.1 and VII.D below) shows that God looks no more favorably on religious pluralism in the eternal state than he does in the present age.

2. The Bible alone is God's Word.

This is demonstrated beginning at II.D below.

3. Jesus Christ alone is God's way of salvation.

This is demonstrated in IV.C.4 and VI.D.2 below.

4. Christians are "inclusive" in the sense that they want all to come to the truth.[50]

a. The large emphasis that theologically conservative Christian churches give both to local and to global missions demonstrates that Christians want to include as many people as possible in God's family.

b. God is "inclusive":

    (1) 1 Timothy 2:3–4—"This is good, and pleases God our Savior, who wants all men to be saved and to come to a knowledge of the truth."

    (2) Isaiah 45:22—"Turn to me and be saved, all you ends of the earth."

    (3) Ezekiel 18:23—"Do I take any pleasure in the death of the wicked? declares the Sovereign LORD. Rather, am I not pleased when they turn from their ways and live?"

c. Jesus is "inclusive":

    (1) Matthew 28:19—"Therefore go and make disciples of all nations."

    (2) John 3:17—"For God did not send his Son into the world to condemn the world, but to save the world through him."

d. Jesus' apostles were "inclusive":

    (1) Acts 26:28–29—"Paul replied, '... I pray God that not only you but all who are listening to me today may become what I am.'"

    (2) Romans 1:16—"I am not ashamed of the gospel, because it is the power of God for the salvation of everyone who believes: first for the Jew, then for the Gentile."

5. The Christian faith has objective content that makes it Christian and not something else.

a. The Christian faith is a definite system of beliefs with definite content (Jude 3).

---

[50]See discussion at C.7 above.

b. Central doctrines include the Trinity, the deity of Christ, the bodily resurrection, the atoning work of Christ on the cross, and salvation by grace through faith.

c. Scripture itself makes it plain that these beliefs are of central importance (e.g., Matt. 28:19; John 8:24 [KJV]; 1 Cor. 15; Eph. 2:8–10).

d. Because the central doctrines define the character of Christianity, one cannot be saved and deny these.

e. Central doctrines should not be confused with peripheral issues, about which Christians may legitimately differ (e.g., mode of baptism, end-time events).

II. Divine Revelation and the Bible

A. *The Unitarian Universalist Positions on Divine Revelation and the Bible Briefly Stated*

1. Reason, conscience, and personal experience are the final judges of all religious truth claims. All religious doctrines that do not conform to these must be rejected.

2. The Bible is but one of many sacred books that may reveal divine truth.

3. Many UUs find inspiring truths in the Bible, while others do not.

4. Like all sacred books, the Bible is not infallible; it is a human book that contains errors.

5. The Bible is not to be interpreted literally.

B. *Arguments Used by Unitarian Universalists to Support Their Views of Divine Revelation and the Bible*

1. Reason, conscience, and personal experience are the final judges of all religious truth claims. All religious doctrines that do not conform to these must be rejected.

a. "We believe that personal experience, conscience and reason should be the final authorities in religion. In the end religious authority lies not in a book or person or institution, but in ourselves."[51]

b. Jack Mendelsohn states, "Reason holds the place that is ordinarily accorded to revelation in orthodox religions."[52]

c. David Rankin observes, "We believe in the authority of reason and conscience."[53]

---

[51]Unitarian Universalist Association, *We Are Unitarian Universalists* (Boston: Unitarian Universalist Association, 1992).

[52]Mendelsohn, *Meet the Unitarian Universalists,* 5. Mendelsohn is the Unitarian minister emeritus of the First Parish in Bedford, Mass.

[53]Rankin, *What Do Unitarian Universalists Believe?* point 3.

2. The Bible is but one of many sacred books that may reveal divine truth.
   a. Edington states, "We regard the Bible as one of many important religious texts but do not consider it unique or exclusive in any way."[54]
   b. Karl Chworowsky and Christopher Raible observe, "Many Unitarian Universalists have a concept of a 'loose-leaf' Bible, that is, they find inspiration in many writings—the scriptures of many religions, the philosophers of many times, the literature of many cultures."[55]
3. Many UUs find inspiring truths in the Bible, while others do not.
   a. Hewett states, "No Unitarian [*sic*] would wish to downplay either the literary beauty or the spiritual insights to be found in parts of the Bible."[56]
   b. Judith Hoehler, a Christian UU feminist, believes that although the Bible was "forged in a patriarchal culture" and is "full of male imagery, male dominance, and male language"—its "core message" is "one of liberation."[57]
   c. Some do not draw inspiration from the Bible, such as some UU humanists,[58] avowedly non-Christian UU feminists, and UU Neopagans.
4. Like all sacred books, the Bible is not infallible; it is a human book that contains errors.
   a. The Bible contains historical errors.
      (1) Delos McKown asserts, "No one of the four Christs of the four gospels is the real Jesus through and through. Those Christs are theological concoctions made up in some part out of historical scraps of information about Jesus but in greater part out of Christian faith and the polemical, apologetic, and idiosyncratic interests of each gospel writer.... The real Jesus can never stand up to our inspection and questioning."[59]
      (2) George Marshall says, "Historically, some of it is a faithful representation of the events recorded, but some of it is wide of the mark."[60]

---

[54]Sias, *100 Questions,* 4. See also Unitarian Universalist Association, "Principles and Purposes," in the *UUA 1997–98 Directory,* 3; and Church, "The Cathedral of the World," in *Our Chosen Faith,* 96.

[55]Chworowsky and Raible, "What Is a Unitarian Universalist?" 266.

[56]Hewett, *The Unitarian Way,* 93. As will be seen, certainly some Unitarians see little if anything of value in the Bible.

[57]Judith L. Hoehler, "The Bible as a Source of Feminist Theology," *Unitarian Universalist Christian* 37, no. 3–4 (Fall/Winter 1982): 21.

[58]For example, see Delos B. McKown, "A Humanist Looks at the Future of Unitarian Universalism," *Religious Humanism* 20, no. 2 (Spring 1986): 59.

[59]Ibid., 62–63.

[60]Marshall, *Challenge of a Liberal Faith,* 152. See also G. Peter Fleck, "Why the Bible is Important to Us," *Unitarian Universalist Christian* 44, no. 1 (Spring 1989): 6.

(3) Barbara Marshman rejects "miracle stories" as "embellishments."[61]

b. The Bible contains textual errors.

Hewett argues that the words of Jesus as we have them today are very inexact and not literally his words, since they represent translations from spoken Aramaic that entered into Greek written records that have in turn been handed down and translated into English.[62]

c. The Bible contains moral and ethical errors.

(1) F. Forrester Church states, "Some [books of the Bible] are dramatically uneven in spiritual quality, the most sublime sentiments coupled with theological and ethical barbarisms in the same text."[63]

(2) Larsen calls certain of Jesus' moral teachings "a lot stricter than I would want to be. Jesus also opposed divorce.... Do any religious liberals agree with that? Or with his teaching that it's even sinful to have sexual *thoughts* about someone?"[64]

5. The Bible is not to be interpreted literally.[65]

a. Edington states flatly, "We do not interpret it literally."[66]

b. Some regard it as a book that teaches inspiring *myths*.

Arvid Straube states, "The Bible is, in its core and essence, a myth ... not bound by the usual limitations of language and able to express many layers of meaning."[67]

C. Refutation of Arguments Used by Unitarian Universalists to Support Their View of Divine Revelation and the Bible

1. The UUs misapply reason in their rejection of orthodox Christian truth.

a. Historic Christian orthodoxy ought not to be rejected as unreasonable. Christian theologians use reason in articulating the faith.

(1) While some Christian truths are "supranatural" (*above* reason) because they can never be known apart from God's revealing them to us, very few Christian theologians have even *attempted* to argue that the Christian faith is irrational or contrary to reason. Suprarational truths are not irrational.

---

[61] Daniel G. Higgins, Jr., et al., *Unitarian Universalist Views of Jesus* (Boston: Unitarian Universalist Association, 1994).

[62] Hewett, *The Unitarian Way*, 92–93.

[63] Church, "Neighborhood," in *Our Chosen Faith*, 127–29.

[64] Larsen and Schmidt, *Catechism*, 9. Larsen indicates (p. 10) that he believes that these and other sayings with which he takes offense are nevertheless genuine teachings of Jesus.

[65] See D.5 below for the proper meaning of the expression "literal interpretation."

[66] Sias, *100 Questions*, 4.

[67] Arvid Straube, "The Bible in Unitarian Universalist Theology," *Unitarian Universalist Christian* 44, no. 1 (1989): 23. See also J. Frank Schulman, "An Affirmation That Life Has Meaning," in *Unitarian Universalist Views of the Bible*, ed. Daniel G. Higgins, Jr. (Boston: Unitarian Universalist Association, 1994).

(2) Any systematic theology, Protestant or Catholic, appeals to rational distinctions and philosophical argumentation (e.g., Thomas Aquinas' *Summa Theologica,* Charles Hodge's *Systematic Theology*).

(3) It is simply not the case that UUs prize rationality while orthodox theologians eschew it. One rarely encounters tightly reasoned, logical argumentation in UU writings, but rather broad, sweeping, sentimental and emotive statements, often vague and offered with no philosophical justification.[68]

b. Orthodox theologians use reason in defining, explaining, and defending the Christian faith, and it is appropriate for them to do so.

(1) Any affirmation that entails an actual logical contradiction cannot be a genuine doctrine of the faith, since (true) faith and (true) reason cohere and do not contradict.

(2) Even in the case of doctrines that we accept by "faith" (i.e., trust), there is good reason to believe that the Bible is an inspired communication from God to the human race.[69] It is reasonable to trust what it says, even in those areas where independent confirmation may not be possible. Biblical faith is not *blind* faith but is faith grounded in God's having demonstrated his truthfulness in the past. Christian belief is not contrary to the evidence, but consistent with it.

c. The type of "reason" used by UUs in rejecting Christian orthodoxy is actually subjective bias, personal preference, or dogmatic assertion.

(1) UUs rarely attempt to demonstrate *why* one should reject the doctrines of historic orthodoxy.

(2) It is clear from UU literature that when UUs describe a doctrine as "unreasonable," they really mean that they personally dislike the doctrine.

(3) For example, UUs reject the miraculous elements of Christianity as unreasonable, but without demonstrating why they are so, or reject the doctrine of hell as "unreasonable," claiming that it "doesn't make sense" for a God of love to consign anyone to eternal perdition.[70]

2. Since one's convictions based on conscience can be unreliable, it ought not to be a final arbiter of religious truth.

a. Scripture indicates that the conscience can be an accurate gauge of moral rectitude (e.g., Acts 23:1; 24:16; Rom. 2:15; 2 Cor. 1:12; 1 Tim.

---

[68]Example: "[We affirm and promote the] direct experience of that transcending mystery and wonder, affirmed in all cultures, which moves us to a renewal of the spirit and an openness to the forces which create and uphold life" (UUA *Statement of Principles and Purposes*).

[69]See the discussion of biblical inspiration at II.D below.

[70]Larsen, "Evangelizing Our Children," in *Salted with Fire,* 128.

1:5, 19; 2 Tim. 1:3; 1 Peter 3:16, 21), particularly for a believer when confirmed by the testimony of the Holy Spirit (Rom. 9:1); but the conscience can also be weak and defiled (1 Cor. 8:7, 10, 12; Titus 1:15), evil (Heb. 10:22), and in need of being purged (Heb. 9:14).

b. Practical experience confirms the Bible's view of the conscience. Some sociopaths have no compunctions whatever about lying, stealing, and even murdering in cold blood.

c. In the sixteenth century the consciences of many non-UUs led them to actively suppress Unitarianism, even to the point of burning Servetus at the stake in Geneva.[71] If conscience can be unreliable in that case (as UUs must surely admit), could it not also be unreliable in others?

3. Religious experience ought not to be a final arbiter of religious truth.[72]

a. Experience does not always entail an infallible interpretation.

(1) The fact of a subjective experience ought not to be confused with one's interpretation of that event's meaning or its correspondence with truth in the external world. For example, a person in a mental institution may "experience" being Napoleon Bonaparte.

(2) A person may experience what he or she considers to be a divine encounter, yet the subjective experience does not demonstrate that as a fact. In some cases it may demonstrate that the person is psychotic.[73]

b. Experience alone cannot be a final arbiter since adherents of contradictory worldviews each cite personal experience in support.

(1) If religions that fundamentally contradict one another all claim subjective experience as their basis, then experience alone cannot be a reliable guide unless we are willing to endure contradictions, which is irrational.

(2) For example, a Mormon (polytheist), a New Ager (pantheist), and a Christian (monotheist) might all claim to have had a divine "experience." Since polytheism, pantheism, and monotheism are mutually exclusive belief systems, at least two of the three must be false, however sincere these individuals' beliefs.

c. The source of the experience may be open to question.

(1) Some experiences may be induced through purely natural means (e.g., drugs, sensory deprivation, imagination).

---

[71]Servetus is discussed at Part I, Section III.B.1 above.

[72]For an interesting discussion on testing the validity of religious experiences, see Norman Geisler and Winfried Corduan, *Philosophy of Religion*, 2d ed. (Grand Rapids: Baker, 1988), 62–76; and Hawkins, *Witchcraft: Exploring the World of Wicca*, 145–50.

[73]For example, see the American Psychiatric Association, *DSM-IV: Diagnostic and Statistical Manual of Mental Disorder*, 4th ed. (Washington, D.C.: American Psychiatric Association, 1994), 297, 301 ("Grandiose Type Delusional Disorder," §297.1).

(2) Other experiences may be induced through paranormal means but could be the products of deception (e.g., demons).

(3) Some experiences might actually be the result of a genuine encounter with the true God of the Bible (see Acts 9:3–8).

(4) A person could have a genuine experience with the true God, but misunderstand and conclude, for example, that God is All or that God is a big man on another planet.

(5) Thus, mere experience is not necessarily sufficient to demonstrate the objective truth of a worldview. It requires other factors, such as a worldview's internal and external consistency.

4. The Bible is qualitatively different from all other so-called sacred books and alone is the Word of God.[74]

a. The Bible's testability distinguishes it from other sacred books.

(1) Unlike the sacred writings of every other religion, the Bible and the Christianity based on it are (at the least in all major essential points) both verifiable and theoretically falsifiable.

(2) Biblical revelation is rooted in history, whereas other sacred writings are based on subjective claims that are untestable. For example, scholars disagree as to when Buddha lived, just what he himself taught, or whether he even lived at all.[75]

(3) In contradistinction to all other religions, Christianity is based on the authority of a *person:* the Lord Jesus Christ. It is not the authority of one who proffers the teaching of another, but one whose truth is grounded in himself. Jesus claimed to be God himself and showed this to be true by rising from the dead.

(4) Because Jesus' claims are rooted in history, they are theoretically *falsifiable.* Jesus claimed that he would rise from the dead, and did so in the presence of many witnesses (including nonbelievers). Had he not actually risen, the enemies of Christianity would have readily falsified Jesus' claims (e.g., by producing his body), as it was clearly in their interest to do so.

b. Because Jesus rose from the dead, his teachings are to be believed.

(1) Jesus' teachings have authority only in so far as he is who he claimed to be, based on the fact that he did what he claimed he would do (i.e., raise himself from the dead [John 2:19]).

(2) Jesus was not simply a purveyor of a system of morals, ethics, or spiritual "truths." Rather, he is the *source* of these teach-

---

[74]For the following subpoints, I am indebted to ideas gained from my discussions with Robert and Gretchen Passantino of Answers in Action.

[75]See F. F. Bruce's insightful comments in *The New Testament Documents: Are They Reliable?* 5th rev. ed. (Grand Rapids: Eerdmans, 1960), 7–8.

ings, which are grounded in him as *truth itself* (John 14:6). The teachings stand or fall with Jesus himself.

(3) Jesus was not executed for what he did or taught, but for who he said he *was*.

5. The Bible is objectively an inspired book, regardless of whatever "inspirations" any particular UU may or may not draw from it.

See the discussion of biblical inspiration under D.1 below.

6. Contrary to the UU claim, the Bible is without error.

a. The UU argument, "The Bible is a human book and so must contain errors" is itself erroneous.

(1) God produced the Bible by using human authors, but also superintended them so as to shield from error what they wrote (2 Peter 1:21).

(2) It would not follow that the Bible is fallible on the grounds it contains statements produced by humans. Indeed, the UU statement, "The Bible is human, therefore fallible" is itself a human statement, yet is offered as true. UUs conveniently (and illogically) exempt their own statements against the Bible from this canon of proof.

b. The Bible does not contain historical errors.[76]

(1) On strictly historical grounds, the Bible is the most reliable book ever penned.

(2) The biblical text that we use today is unusually well attested; we can have high confidence that the Bible we possess today reflects almost exactly the original. (See discussion below.)

(3) We have good reasons for trusting the truthfulness and reliability of the accounts furnished by the biblical writers.

Consider the Gospels: Men who knew Jesus personally and who were eyewitnesses of his life and ministry wrote them. These same men were willing to suffer persecution and in some cases be put to death for their testimony.[77]

---

[76]The following books deal with purported historical discrepancies in the Bible: Gleason Archer, *Encyclopedia of Bible Difficulties* (Grand Rapids: Zondervan, 1982); and Norman Geisler and Thomas Howe, *When Critics Ask* (Wheaton, Ill.: Scripture Press, 1992). See also Norman Geisler and William Nix, *A General Introduction to the Bible* (Chicago: Moody Press, 1968; rev. and expanded 1986), 52, 55–64. For a defense of the archaeological trustworthiness of the Old Testament, see Edwin Yamauchi, *The Stones and the Scriptures* (Philadelphia: J. B. Lippincott, 1972); and Kenneth A. Kitchen, *Ancient Orient and the Old Testament* (Chicago: InterVarsity Press, 1966). Similarly, the historicity of Acts is persuasively argued in I. Howard Marshall, *Luke: Historian and Theologian* (Grand Rapids: Zondervan, 1970); and William M. Ramsay, *St. Paul: The Traveler and the Roman Citizen* (Grand Rapids: Baker, 1962).

[77]See Craig Blomberg, *The Historical Reliability of the Gospels* (Downers Grove, Ill.: InterVarsity Press, 1987); Paul Barnett, *Is the New Testament History?* (Ann Arbor: Servant, 1986); R. T. France, *The Evidence for Jesus*, ed. Michael Green (Downers Grove, Ill.: InterVarsity Press, 1986), esp. 93–139; and Gary R. Habermas, *The Historical Jesus: Ancient Evidence for the Life of Christ* (Joplin, Mo.: College Press, 1996), esp. the summary on 243–55 and the concise outline of the evidence on 275–85.

   c. Contrary to UU critics, the text of the New and Old Testaments that we have today corresponds almost exactly to the original.[78]

     (1) Of the New Testament text, F. F. Bruce states, "The evidence for our New Testament writings is ever so much greater than the evidence for many writings of classical authors, the authenticity of which no-one dreams of questioning. And if the New Testament were a collection of secular writings, their authenticity would generally be regarded as beyond all doubt."[79]

     (2) Even though we have many fewer extant manuscripts when compared to the New Testament, "the Old Testament text owes its accuracy to the ability and reliability of the scribes who transmitted it."[80] For example, "only certain kinds of skins could be used, the size of columns was regulated and the ritual a scribe followed in copying a manuscript followed religious rules. If a manuscript was found to contain even one mistake, it was discarded and destroyed."[81]

     (3) The biblical text has strong external evidence. For example, the writings of the early church fathers provide direct citations and allusions to biblical texts, further supporting the Bible's textual reliability.[82]

   d. The Bible does not contain moral errors.

     (1) What the UUs call "moral errors" in the Bible are simply doctrines of which they disapprove.[83]

     (2) When UUs indict the Bible as ethically inferior—for example, when the Bible condemns sex outside of marriage[84]—they provide no evidence why we should accept their standard of morality by which to judge the Bible. They are sunk in the quagmire of pure subjectivity.

     (3) Jesus Christ attests to the truth of Scripture (Matt. 5:18; Luke 24:25; John 10:35; 17:17) and therefore to any moral pronouncements that it contains, with the authority that comes with his having risen from the dead. None of the UU writers

---

[78]On the reliability of the Old Testament text see Geisler and Nix, *From God to Us*, 138–44; Geisler and Nix, *A General Introduction to the Bible*, 357–82; and Gleason Archer, *A Survey of Old Testament Introduction* (Chicago: Moody Press, 1974), esp. 37–80, 165–76. For a study written by a nonevangelical that likewise supports the reliability of the OT text, see Emanuel Tov, *Textual Criticism of the Hebrew Bible* (Minneapolis: Fortress, 1992). On the New Testament, in addition to the sources cited earlier, see Geisler and Nix, *A General Introduction to the Bible*, 385–408; and Bruce M. Metzger, *The Text of the New Testament* (New York: Oxford, 1968).

[79]Bruce, *The New Testament Documents*, 15.

[80]Norman L. Geisler and William E. Nix, *From God to Us: How We Got Our Bible* (Chicago: Moody Press, 1974), 141.

[81]Ibid. See also Ellis R. Brotzmann, *Old Testament Textual Criticism: A Practical Introduction* (Grand Rapids: Baker, 1994), 62.

[82]Bruce, *The New Testament Documents*, 18.

[83]See II.C.1.c above.

[84]For example, see the complaint of McKown, "A Humanist Looks at the Future of Unitarian Universalism," 62.

who criticize biblical morality can speak with that compelling kind of authority.

7. The Bible is to be interpreted literally—that is, according to the normal conventions of language, history, and culture. (See D.5 below.)

8. The Unitarian Universalist view of the Bible is inconsistent with their use of it to defend their positions.

   a. UUs are sometimes quick to quote the Bible when they believe it agrees with their positions. Yet, given their view of Scripture's deficiencies, they are hardly consistent in doing so.

   b. For example, Hewett tells us that the text of Scripture is massively corrupt, yet draws on this same "corrupt" text to prove that Jesus' Sermon on the Mount teaches the virtue of "inclusiveness" and bases his argument on a close reading of the original language.[85]

D. The Biblical View of Divine Revelation and the Bible

1. The Bible is an inspired book.

   a. The meaning of *biblical inspiration*

      (1) 2 Timothy 3:16 states that all Scripture is "given by inspiration of God" (KJV), or, as the NIV renders it, is "God-breathed." The Greek word *theopneustos* literally means "God-breathed."

      (2) Inspiration refers to the *result* of God's superintendence of the biblical writers (2 Peter 1:21), such that the record they produced was precisely what God wished them to record.

      (3) 2 Timothy 3:16 describes the *Bible* and not the biblical writers per se as inspired.

   b. Because the Bible is God-breathed, it is without error (see below).

2. The Bible is an infallible book, without error.

   a. God's Word is the "word of truth" (Pss. 119:43, 160; 138:2; John 17:17; 2 Cor. 6:7; Eph. 1:13; Col. 1:5; 2 Tim. 2:15; James. 1:18).

   b. Since 2 Timothy 3:16 declares *all* Scripture to be useful, it follows that it is without error, otherwise at least *some* portions would have to be disregarded.

   c. Matthew 5:18—Even the seemingly least significant part (i.e., "jot and tittle") of God's Word stands firm.

   d. Luke 24:25—Jesus chided his disciples as foolish for not believing everything that the prophets had spoken.

   e. John 10:35—Jesus declared that the Scripture cannot be broken.

3. The Bible is the authoritative Word of God.

   a. Because the Bible is a true communication to us from God, it is therefore authoritative because God has authority over us.

   b. God confirmed the authority of his Word by miraculous signs (Mark 16:20; Acts 14:3; Heb. 2:3–4).

---

[85]Hewett, *The Unitarian Way*, 92–93.

49

    c. Joshua 1:7–8—We are to observe God's Word, not turning from it "to the right or to the left."

    d. Matthew 28:19–20—Jesus' disciples are to obey all of his commandments.

4. Because the Bible is authoritative, it is the standard by which any other so-called revelations must be judged.

    a. Acts 17:11—The Bereans tested Paul's teaching against the Old Testament. They understood that any teaching that claimed to be from God had to be consistent with what God already taught.

    b. Deuteronomy 13:1–5—Anyone who claims to be a prophet but contradicts God's Word is to be rejected.

    c. Isaiah 8:20—Those who do not speak according to God's Word have no light in them.

5. The Bible is to be interpreted literally.[86]

    a. The meaning of *literal interpretation*

        (1) A literal interpretation of the Bible means that it is to be understood under the normal rules and conventions of language.

        (2) Literal interpretation takes into account figures of speech and symbolic language and also the historical and cultural context.

            (a) For example, when Jesus states that he is the "gate" for the sheep (John 10:7), a literal interpretation does not picture Jesus as being made of wood and having hinges.

            (b) Thus, in context, the plain meaning of John 10:7 is that Jesus is the one through whom salvation comes. This is what a literal or plain interpretation of the text affirms.

    b. Jesus himself interpreted the Old Testament—the portion of the Bible available in his day—literally. That is, Jesus accepted the Old Testament according to its plain meaning.

    Ron Rhodes points out that Jesus "consistently interpreted the Old Testament in a nonsymbolic, literal way—including the Creation account of Adam and Eve (Matt. 13:35; 25:34; Mark 10:6), Noah's Ark and the Flood (Matt. 24:38–39; Luke 17:26–27), Jonah and the whale (Matt. 12:39–41), Sodom and Gomorrah (Matt. 10:15), and the account of Lot (Luke 17:28–29)."[87]

6. The Bible is not a myth.

    a. There are various definitions for the word *myth*. It appears that what the UUs intend is that the Bible contains "stories" that con-

---

[86]On biblical interpretation, see Gordon D. Fee and Douglas Stuart, *How to Read the Bible for All Its Worth*, 2d ed. (Grand Rapids: Zondervan, 1993). For a more technical work, see Grant R. Osborne, *The Hermeneutical Spiral: A Comprehensive Introduction to Biblical Interpretation* (Downers Grove, Ill.: InterVarsity Press, 1991). See also Leland Ryken, *Words of Delight: A Literary Introduction to the Bible* (Grand Rapids: Baker, 1987).

[87]Ron Rhodes, *New Age Movement*, 34–35.

vey certain spiritual truths in symbolic language, but that these stories are not grounded in actual historical events.

b. Unlike myths that were common in the Graeco-Roman world (e.g., Mithras, Isis and Osiris, Dionysius), "in Christianity everything is made to turn on a dated experience of a historical Person."[88]

c. Additionally, the Bible itself denies that it is a myth (2 Tim. 4:4; 2 Peter 1:16);[89] this shows that the biblical writers did not intend their words to be interpreted in a mythical fashion.

d. It is clear that the biblical writers were offering eyewitness testimony to historical truth. They condemned those who told fanciful stories.[90]

III. The Doctrines of God

A. Unitarian Universalist Positions on God Briefly Stated[91]

1. UUs tolerate a wide diversity of views within their ranks about God.

2. Some UUs do not believe in God at all.

3. Other UUs define God (in whole or in part) as a higher power or "divine spark" within themselves.

4. Some UUs believe "God" is the term for an ordering principle in nature.

5. Process theology is one popular view of God held by many UUs.

6. A Neo-pagan view of God (or the goddess) is becoming an increasingly popular option among UUs.

7. All UUs reject the orthodox doctrine of the Trinity.

B. Arguments Used by Unitarian Universalists to Support Their Doctrines of God

1. UUs tolerate a wide diversity of views about God in their ranks.

a. "Because Unitarian Universalism is a non-creedal religion, all Unitarian Universalists must decide whether or not the concept of God is a central part of their personal religion."[92]

---

[88]Edwin M. Yamauchi, quoting A. D. Nock, in "Easter—Myth, Hallucination, or History?" (Part 1 of 2), *Christianity Today,* 15 March 1974, 6.

[89]Note the use of the Greek word *muthos* in these verses, which means a tale, story, legend, myth, or fable. See William F. Arndt and F. Wilbur Gingrich, *A Greek-English Lexicon of the New Testament and Other Early Christian Literature* (Chicago: University of Chicago, 1957), 530. Hereafter cited as *BAG.*

[90]See William Lane Craig, "Did Jesus Rise from the Dead?" in *Jesus Under Fire,* eds. Michael J. Wilkins and J. P. Moreland (Grand Rapids: Zondervan, 1995), 154.

[91]I have selected only a sampling of UU views of God, realizing that many more positions could be included. For example, New Age views are increasing in favor (see Part I, Section V.B.2. above), but I treat them only indirectly in this section in so far as I refute pantheism generally. Other books, including some in this series, may be consulted for a refutation of positions found in the UU that are not examined here.

[92]Paul H. Beattie, "Personal Choice," in *Unitarian Universalist Views of God,* ed. Doris Hunter (Boston: Unitarian Universalist Association, n.d.), 9.

b. "Unitarian Universalists believe that all persons must decide about God for themselves. In their churches are agnostics, humanists, even atheists—as well as nature worshippers, pantheists, and those who affirm a personal God."[93]

2. Some UUs do not believe in God at all.

a. In a 1989 survey, 18 percent of the UUs surveyed said the concept of God was "irrelevant," and 2 percent called it "harmful."[94]

b. Paul Beattie says, "God, for me, is a word that has outlived its usefulness, and reinterpreting it no longer seems worth the effort."[95]

c. In church life, Edington states, "In most services, there are few, if any, mentions of a deity. The emphasis is on issues of human growth, human potential and personal human issues that we all face in day-to-day living."[96]

3. Other UUs define God (in whole or in part) as a higher power or "divine spark" within themselves.

a. Marshall says, "The objective God 'out there' is not only dead, but the God who is separable from the individual consciousness, from the mind and existence of the individual is also not conceivable."[97]

b. Edington states, "Many believe in a spirit of life or a power within themselves, which some choose to call God."[98]

4. Some UUs believe "God" is the term for an ordering principle in nature.

Arthur Foote states, "The term 'God' for me, therefore, does not mean a Supreme Being, a Divine Person; it is rather my affirmation that the universe and life have some principle of coherence and rationality."[99]

5. Process theology is one popular view of God held by many UUs.

a. David Parke says, "The concept of a changeable God ... attracted wide interest in the [UU] churches," and concludes that process thought "has become perhaps the most representative theological position in contemporary Unitarian Universalism."[100]

b. The "Unitarian Universalist Process Theology Network" propagates process thought within the UU denomination.[101]

---

[93]Chworowsky and Raible, "What Is a Unitarian Universalist?" 265.

[94]UUA, *The Quality of Religious Life in Unitarian Universalist Congregations,* 34, 45.

[95]Beattie, "Personal Choice," 10.

[96]Sias, *100 Questions,* 3.

[97]Marshall, *Challenge of a Liberal Faith,* 140.

[98]Sias, *100 Questions,* 2–3.

[99]Arthur Foote, "The Heart of Reality," in *Unitarian Universalist Views of God,* 2.

[100]David B. Parke, "Theological Directions of Unitarian Universalism for the Next 25 Years," *Unitarian Universalist Christian* 44 nos. 3–4 (1989): 11–12.

[101]*UUA 1997–98 Directory,* 408.

6. A Neo-pagan view of God (or the goddess) is becoming an increasingly popular option among UUs.[102]

   a. For examples in the UUA hymnbook, see Part I, Section V.B.3.d.[103]

   b. One also finds hymns reflecting Native American spirituality, such as the Tewa Indian's "O Our Mother the Earth" and the Navajo "Beauty is Before Me."[104]

   c. The Covenant of Unitarian Universalist Pagans (CUUPS) is an active, growing group within the UUA.

7. All UUs reject the orthodox doctrine of the Trinity.

   a. Historically, Unitarian Universalism rejected the doctrine of the Trinity as illogical and unscriptural.[105]

   b. Modern UUs have little interest in the doctrine of the Trinity, but when they do consider it, they reject it.

      (1) Joseph Bassett notes that there is a "lack of continuing interest in such doctrines."[106]

      (2) Chworowsky and Raible state, "In general, Unitarian Universalists believe in the oneness of reality and think of God as a unity rather than a trinity."[107]

C. *Refutation of Arguments Used by Unitarian Universalists to Support Their Doctrines of God*

1. Contrary to the teaching of atheist UUs, God does exist.

   a. Not only does the Bible affirm God's existence (see D.1 below), but there are excellent philosophical reasons for affirming it as well.[108]

   b. Christian (and even non-Christian) philosophers have provided excellent arguments and evidence for God's existence. For example, Thomas Aquinas developed five credible proofs for God's existence that are still taken seriously by philosophers today.[109]

---

[102]See Part I, V.B.3 above. See also Margot Adler, *Drawing Down the Moon* (Boston: Beacon, 1986), 435–36.

[103]See James, *Between the Lines: Sources for Singing the Living Tradition*, 103, 116, 117.

[104]Ibid., 116, 142.

[105]See Part I, Section I.B.1 above.

[106]Joseph A. Bassett, "In and About the Vineyard [Ecumenical notes]," *Unitarian Universalist Christian* 43 no. 1 (1988): 46.

[107]Chworowsky and Raible, "What Is a Unitarian Universalist?" 263–64.

[108]As an introduction, the reader should consult the contemporary exchange between J. P. Moreland, a Christian theist philosopher, and Kai Nielsen, an atheist philosopher (*Does God Exist? The Debate between Theists and Atheists* [Buffalo: Prometheus Books, 1993]). For other good, recent philosophical works arguing for God's existence, see Richard Swinburne, *The Existence of God*, rev. ed. (New York: Oxford, 1991); Richard Swinburne, *Is There a God?* (New York: Oxford, 1996); and William Lane Craig, *Reasonable Faith* (Wheaton, Ill.: Crossway, 1994).

[109]For an older but very insightful discussion of these proofs by a major Aquinas scholar, see Etienne Gilson, *The Christian Philosophy of St. Thomas Aquinas* (New York: Random House, 1956), 59–83.

    c. Some of the philosophical arguments that demonstrate or lend credence to God's existence are the following:[110]

      (1) The *cosmological* argument, which argues from the impossibility of an infinite regress;[111]

      (2) The *teleological* argument, which argues that the order and structure we see in the universe implies an intelligent mind who structured it;

      (3) The *ontological* argument, which affirms that since God is a being than which no greater can be conceived, God must really exist, for to exist in the mind alone is not as great as to exist in reality;

      (4) The *moral* argument, which starts with the fact that people have an innate sense of right and wrong and then moves to the notion that our innate sense of morality is derived from a moral lawgiver.

2. God is not a higher power or "divine spark" within human beings.

    a. The notion that God is a higher power within humanity fails to distinguish properly between God and his creation.

    b. This idea depersonalizes God, making him a "power" rather than a person.

    c. No evidence is offered for why we should think of God in this way. When Marshall states dogmatically that a God who is external to us is "inconceivable," he provides no arguments for the assertion.

    d. That God is not a higher power or "divine spark" within humans is shown by the fact that humans do not manifest the attributes of divinity. (See discussion in IV.C.1 below.)

3. "God" is not the term for the ordering principle in nature.

    a. Again, to speak of God as a "principle" denies that God is personal.

    b. While it is true that God "orders" the realm of nature (Heb. 1:3) as its creator and sustainer (Gen. 1:1; Ps. 102:25; Isa. 45:12, 18; John 1:3; Col. 1:16–17; Heb. 1:3; 3:3–4; Rev. 4:11), it does not follow that he is the ordering principle itself, any more than an engineer who designs and builds a machine is to be confused with the laws and principles that make the machine function (Heb. 3:3–4).

    c. God's transcendence from creation is discussed at D.6.

4. Process theology is to be rejected.[112]

---

[110]These are briefly summarized in Wayne Grudem, *Systematic Theology* (Grand Rapids: Zondervan, 1994), 143–44. I have followed some of his explanations and modified others.

[111]For a detailed discussion, see J. P. Moreland, *Scaling the Secular City* (Grand Rapids: Baker, 1987), 15–42.

[112]For a substantive critique of process thought at the hands of several top Christian theologians and philosophers, see Ronald H. Nash, ed., *Process Theology* (Grand Rapids: Baker, 1987).

    a. Christians classically have affirmed God's immutability, the denial of which is the central tenet of process theology.[113]

    b. God's immutability is discussed at D.5.

5. The Neo-pagan view of God (or the goddess) is false.

    a. The Neo-pagan position is riddled with philosophical, ethical, and theological problems.[114]

    b. Some Neo-pagans hold to a pantheistic view of God.[115] (See D.6.)

    c. Other Neo-pagans hold to a polytheistic view of God. (See D.2.)

6. The doctrine of the Trinity is true.

God's triunity—that within the nature of the one God there are three eternal persons, Father, Son, and Holy Spirit—is taught clearly in Scripture. (See D.4.)

D. The Biblical Doctrine of God

1. God exists.

    a. The Bible both teaches and assumes God's existence as an undeniable fact, beginning with Genesis 1:1.

    b. On the basis of Scripture and experience, the psalmist charges that only a fool would deny God's existence (Pss. 14:1; 53:1).

    c. God's existence is evident even to those who have not had access to the Bible, through what he has created (Ps. 19:1–2; Acts 14:17; Rom. 1:19–20), however much people may suppress that truth (Rom. 1:21–23).

2. There is only one God.

The Bible is exceedingly clear that there is only one true God.

    a. Deuteronomy 6:4—"Hear, O Israel: The LORD our God, the LORD is one."

    b. Isaiah 43:10—"Before me no god was formed, nor will there be one after me."

    c. Isaiah 46:9—"I am God, and there is no other; I am God, and there is none like me."

    d. 1 Corinthians 8:4–6—"There is no God but one. For even if there are so-called gods ... yet for us there is but one God, the Father."

---

[113]A good defense of the classic doctrine of God's immutability is found in Richard A. Muller, "Incarnation, Immutability, and the Case for Classical Theism," *Westminster Theological Journal* 45 (1983): 22–40. See also Bruce Ware, "An Exposition and Critique of the Process Doctrines of Divine Mutability and Immutability," *Westminster Theological Journal* 47 (1985): 175–96; and "An Evangelical Reformulation of the Doctrine of the Immutability of God," *Journal of the Evangelical Theological Society* 29 (1986): 431–46.

[114]Some Neo-pagans hold multiple—even mutually exclusive—views of God at the same time. See Hawkins, *Goddess Worship, Witchcraft and Neo-Paganism*, 42–43. See also his *Witchcraft: Exploring the World of Wicca.*

[115]For a recent critique of pantheism, see David K. Clark and Norman L. Geisler, *Apologetics in the New Age: A Christian Critique of Pantheism* (Grand Rapids: Baker, 1990).

      e. 1 Timothy 2:5—"For there is one God."

  3. God is personal.

      a. Wayne Grudem observes that God interacts with us personally, "and we can relate to him as persons."[116]

      b. Activities are ascribed to God that apply only to persons:

         (1) God loves (e.g., Ex. 34:6; Deut. 7:9; 1 Kings 10:9; 2 Chron. 6:14, 42; 9:8; Neh. 1:5; 9:17, 32; 13:22).

         (2) God speaks (e.g., Num. 23:19; 1 Sam. 2:30; Job 33:14; Ps. 50:7).[117]

         (3) God knows, understands, and thinks (e.g., Gen. 3:5; 1 Sam. 2:3; 1 Chron. 28:9; Pss. 37:13; 44:21; 94:9–11; 138:6; Luke 16:15).

         (4) God hates (e.g., wickedness) (Deut. 12:31; 16:22; 22:5; 23:18; 25:16; Pss. 11:5; 45:7; Prov. 6:16).

         (5) God grieves (Gen. 6:6; Eph. 4:30).

         (6) God rejoices (Isa. 62:5).

  4. God is triune.

When orthodox Christians affirm that God is triune, they mean that the one God exists as three eternal persons: the Father, the Son, and the Holy Spirit. The three persons are not three gods, but one God.[118]

      a. There is only one God (see D.2 above).

      b. A person called the Father is God—"God the Father" (e.g., John 6:27; 1 Cor. 8:6; Gal. 1:1, 3; Eph. 6:23; Phil. 2:11; 1 Thess. 1:1).

      c. A person called the Son is God.

The Bible explicitly affirms Jesus' deity, even calling him "God" in many passages.[119]

      d. A person called the Holy Spirit is God.

         (1) Acts 5:3–4—When Ananias lied to the Holy Spirit, he lied to God.

         (2) Passages that present the triune formula of "Father, Son, and Holy Spirit" show that the Holy Spirit is on the same level as Father and Son. Many passages treat the three as coordinate (e.g., Matt. 28:19; 1 Cor. 12:4–6; 2 Cor. 13:14; Eph. 4:4–6; 1 Peter 1:2; Jude 20–21).

         (3) The Spirit is God because he has the attributes that belong to God alone, such as omniscience (1 Cor. 2:10–11) and omnipresence (Ps. 139:7–8).

---

[116]Grudem, *Systematic Theology*, 167.

[117]Many Scripture passages contain the words "the Lord declares" or "thus saith the Lord."

[118]One might argue, as the *Watchtower* does, that the same word "God" is used equivocally: The term "God" means one thing when applied to the Father (i.e., Almighty God by nature) but means another thing when applied to the Son (i.e., a powerful creature). For a refutation of this, see Robert M. Bowman, Jr., *Jehovah's Witnesses* (Grand Rapids: Zondervan, 1995), 24–25, in this series.

[119]For proof that Jesus Christ, the Son of God, is also God by nature, see IV.D.1 below.

5. God is immutable.[120] Contrary to the god of process theology, the God of the Bible is unchanging in his being and in the character and decisions that flow from that being.

   a. Psalm 102:25–27; Hebrews 1:10–12—Even though created things change, including passing into and out of existence, God himself remains the same.

   b. Malachi 3:6—God states explicitly that he does not change.

   c. James 1:17—There is no changeableness in God.

   d. Psalm 33:11; Isaiah 46:9–11; Numbers 23:19—God's counsels stand forever (cf. 1 Sam. 15:29). What he has decreed, he will surely bring to pass.

   e. Numbers 23:19—Unlike human beings, who are often fickle, God never changes his mind (cf. 1 Sam. 15:29).[121]

6. God is transcendent and separate from his creation.

   See Marshall's statement in Section III.B.3.a above and contrast it with the teachings of the inspired biblical writers:

   a. Solomon had no problem conceiving of an objective God "out there" (1 Kings 8:27; Eccl. 5:2).

   b. Moses could conceive of an objective God "out there" (Gen. 1:1).

   c. Isaiah could conceive of an objective God "out there" (Isa. 55:8–9).

   d. David could conceive of an objective God "out there" (Pss. 57:5, 11; 108:5; 139:2).

   e. God himself has no problem conceiving of an objective God "out there" (Ezek. 28:1–2).

7. God is immanent (actively involved) in his creation.

   a. Job 12:10—All living things depend on God for continuing life.

   b. Acts 17:25, 28—Paul affirms not only that God is the author of all life, but also that he continually sustains that life.

   c. Colossians 1:17; Hebrews 1:3—In Christ "all things hold together"; he sustains all things by his powerful word.

IV. The Doctrines of Christ (Christology)

A. The Unitarian Universalist Positions on Jesus Christ Briefly Stated

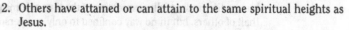

1. Jesus Christ was not divine in any special sense.

2. Others have attained or can attain to the same spiritual heights as Jesus.

---

[120]For a response to process theology, see the two articles by Ware cited in note 113 above.

[121]Some have tried to argue that God changes his mind, basing their argument on passages such as the one in which God relents on his threat to punish the Ninevites (Jonah 3:4, 10). For a detailed discussion of such texts see Alan W. Gomes, "God in Man's Image: Freedom, Foreknowledge, and the 'Openness' of God," *Christian Research Journal* 10, no. 1 (Summer 1987): 18–24.

3. Christ's miracles, virgin birth, and bodily resurrection are to be rejected.

4. Like all human teachers, Jesus should not be seen as infallible or taken as the final authority.

5. Many UUs regard Jesus as one of the world's great ethical teachers.

6. Some UUs reject Jesus even as an ethical model to follow.

B. *Arguments Used by Unitarian Universalists to Support Their Positions on Jesus Christ*

1. Jesus Christ was not divine in any special sense.

   a. Chworowsky and Raible ask, "Do Unitarian Universalists think that Jesus Christ was divine? ... In a sense they think that every person is divine—that is, that there is goodness and worth in everyone. Some call it a 'divine spark,' others simply 'human dignity.' However, Unitarian Universalists see no need for the concept of a special divinity in Christ."[122]

   b. Richard M. Fewkes argues, "The divinity in Jesus points to the divinity in all human persons. It is not a supernatural essence which raises Jesus to a higher level of being above the rest of humanity. A difference in degree, perhaps, but not a difference in kind of nature.... Whatever is true about Jesus is true about each of us in general, at least potentially. This is basic to any Unitarian Universalist understanding of the Incarnation or divinity of Christ."[123]

2. Others have attained or can attain to the same spiritual heights of Jesus.

   a. Sometimes UUs speak in general terms of how others may attain to the spiritual stature as Jesus.

   Hewett writes, "Unitarians believe that outstanding personages such as Jesus and Socrates and the Buddha are part of our common humanity, not intrusions from the outside. They attain heights that can be reached also by others within this same common humanity, and no doubt have been on many occasions."[124]

   b. Some UUs speak in terms of "the Christ" as a divine principle or consciousness, particularly embodied in the man Jesus but capable of being embodied in us.

      (1) Hewett believes others can attain the Christ consciousness that Jesus did: "The Christ-spirit is therefore a universal feature of human life, finding fuller expression in the lives of some persons than of others, but in no way confined to only one person."[125]

---

[122]Chworowsky and Raible, "What Is a Unitarian Universalist?" 267.

[123]Cited in Higgins, *Unitarian Universalist Views of Jesus.*

[124]Hewett, *The Unitarian Way,* 89.

[125]Ibid., 90.

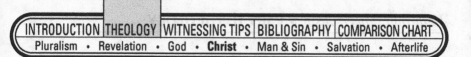
(2) Paul Trudinger believes that Jesus was indwelt by the Christ.[126]

3. Christ's miracles, virgin birth, and bodily resurrection are to be rejected.

   a. Chworowsky and Raible: "Unitarian Universalists emphatically reject them [the Virgin Birth and bodily resurrection] as contrary to both scientific and historical evidence."[127]

   b. Marshman states, "I approach the miracle stories as an embellishment to heighten interest in the life of a good man."[128]

4. Like all human teachers, Jesus should not be seen as infallible or taken as the final authority.

   a. Chworowsky and Raible: "In general, Unitarian Universalists . . . honor the ethical leadership of Jesus without considering him to be their final religious authority."[129]

   b. Larsen is even more pointed in his disclaimer: "If I had been around in Jesus' time . . . I'm not so sure I would have become a disciple. I think he had some very mistaken ideas about himself and the world. . . . Jesus seemed to believe God was working in a special way through *him* to bring about the kingdom of heaven. And I tend to get suspicious right away of anyone who claims to be God's unique vehicle or messenger."[130]

5. Many UUs regard Jesus Christ as one of the world's great ethical teachers.

   a. "Most UUs view Jesus as a moral and ethical teacher and no more than that. . . . Most UUs regard Jesus as one of a number of especially gifted, insightful teachers of humanity."[131]

   b. "[UUs] are inspired by the life and teachings of Jesus as an extraordinary fellow human being."[132]

6. Some UUs reject Jesus even as an ethical model to follow.

   a. McKown says that "the better we get to know the historical Jesus, the less we shall admire him."[133]

   b. McKown decries Jesus' teachings as ethically inferior on issues such as sexual morality, divorce, and his role as redeemer.[134]

[126]Paul Trudinger, "St. Paul: A Unitarian Universalist Christian?" *Faith and Freedom* 43 (Spr-Sum 1990): 57.

[127]Chworowsky and Raible, "What Is a Unitarian Universalist?" 267; see also Sias, *100 Questions,* 3–4, 6.

[128]Cited in Higgins, *Unitarian Universalist Views of Jesus.*

[129]Chworowsky and Raible, "What Is a Unitarian Universalist?" 263–64.

[130]Larsen and Schmidt, *Catechism,* 9.

[131]Sias, *100 Questions,* 6, 21.

[132]Chworowsky and Raible, "What Is a Unitarian Universalist?" 265, 267.

[133]McKown, "A Humanist Looks at the Future of Unitarian Universalism," 59.

[134]Ibid., 62–63. Larsen makes this same point. See Larsen and Schmidt, *Catechism,* 9.

C. Refutation of Arguments Used by Unitarian Universalists to Support Their Positions on Jesus Christ

1. Jesus is divine in a unique, special sense, whereas we are not divine.

   a. Contrary to the claims of some UUs, we are not divine, while Jesus of Nazareth was and is. (For proof that Jesus is uniquely God, see D.1 below.)

   b. The word *divine* can be used in a loose sense (e.g., to have godlike qualities) or in a strict sense (e.g., to be deity).[135] Jesus is God in both senses. (See Col. 2:9.)

   c. None of us is God by nature, nor do we manifest godlike qualities.[136]

      (1) Ezekiel 28:2, 9b—"This is what the Sovereign LORD says: 'In the pride of your heart you say, "I am a god; I sit on the throne of a god in the heart of the seas."' But you are a man and not a god, though you think you are as wise as a god.... You will be but a man, not a god, in the hands of those who slay you."

      (2) Isaiah 42:8; 48:11—God will not share his glory with another.

   d. Ron Rhodes points out some of the many differences between what we would expect to see if we really were divine and the way we actually are:[137]

      (1) God is *all-knowing* (Matt. 19:26), but man is limited in knowledge (Job 38:1–4).

      (2) God is *all-powerful* (Rev. 19:6), but man is weak (Heb. 4:15).

      (3) God is *everywhere-present* (Ps. 139:7–12), but man is confined to a single space at a time (e.g., John 1:50).

      (4) God is *holy* (Rev. 4:8), but (fallen) man's "righteous" deeds are as filthy garments before God (Isa. 64:6).

      (5) God is *eternal* (Ps. 90:2), but man was created at a point in time (Gen. 1:1, 21, 26–27).

      (6) God is *truth* (John 14:6), but (fallen) man's heart is deceitful above all else (Jer. 17:9).

      (7) God is characterized by *justice* (Acts 17:31), but (fallen) man is lawless (1 John 3:4; cf. Rom. 3:23).

      (8) God is *love* (1John 4:16), but (fallen) man is plagued with many vices like jealousy and strife (1 Cor. 3:3).

2. No one will attain to the spiritual status of Jesus, either in this life or the next.

   a. Jesus' sinlessness is proof positive that no one will ever attain to his spiritual heights in this life.

---

[135]For example, see *The American Heritage Dictionary,* 2d College Ed., s.v. "divine."

[136]See also Acts 14:11, 14–15 and Psalm 82:6–7.

[137]See Rhodes, *New Age Movement,* 60–61.

(1) The more sinful a person is, the less spiritual he or she is (at least in the sense of true, biblical spirituality).

(2) Jesus Christ was the sinless Son of God (John 8:29, 46; 2 Cor. 5:21; Heb. 4:15; 7:26; 1 Peter 1:19; 2:22).

(3) All other humans are sinful (1 Kings 8:46; Pss. 14:1–4; 143:2; Prov. 20:9; Eccl. 7:20; Isa. 53:6; Rom. 5:12; 3:23; Gal. 3:22; James 3:2; 1 John 1:8, 10[138]).

b. Jesus' unique sonship demonstrates that no one could ever attain to Jesus' spiritual stature, even in heaven.

(1) Although we will be sinless in heaven (1 Thess. 5:23; Rev. 21:27), we will still never be as "spiritually attuned" as Jesus.

(2) Contrary to UU claims, Jesus' sonship is altogether unique.

(3) The apostle John describes Jesus as the "one and only Son" of God (e.g., John 1:14, 18; 3:16, 18; 1 John 4:9).[139]

c. Contrary to UU claims, Jesus' "Christhood" is not a divine principle or consciousness, embodied in him but manifest in others.

(1) This is a fundamental error of the New Age movement, the mind sciences, and certain forms of ancient Gnosticism.

(2) The Scriptures make it quite clear that Jesus is not indwelt by some kind of "Christ principle" but that he is himself the Christ (Matt. 16:16; 26:63–64; Luke 2:11; John 1:41; 11:27).[140]

(3) If Jesus were merely indwelt by a "Christ principle" or "christ consciousness" while claiming to *be* the only Christ, such indwelling had little practical value in helping Jesus to form an accurate spiritual self-assessment.

3. Christ's miracles, virgin birth, and bodily resurrection actually occurred and therefore should be accepted.[141]

a. The writers of Scripture give eyewitness testimony to miraculous occurrences and the fact of the bodily resurrection.

b. Of the resurrection, Bruce states, "we are confronted with a hard core of historical fact: (a) the tomb was really empty; (b) the Lord appeared to various individuals and groups of disciples both in Judaea and in Galilee; (c) the Jewish authorities could not disprove the disciples' claim that He had risen from the dead."[142]

---

[138]In these verses John used the first person plural ("we"), acknowledging his sinfulness.

[139]The word translated "one and only" is *monogenes* in Greek, which is more properly rendered "unique; one of a kind." See *BAG*, "*monogenes*," 529.

[140]See also the discussion in Rhodes, *New Age Movement*, 52–53, 56.

[141]On the reliability of the Gospels in general and for the historicity of the resurrection in particular, see Habermas, *The Historical Jesus: Ancient Evidence for the Life of Christ*. On the miracles of Jesus, see also Gary Habermas, "Did Jesus Perform Miracles?" in *Jesus Under Fire*, 117–40.

[142]Bruce, *The New Testament Documents*, 65.

    c. The resurrection stories of Christ have the earmarks of authenticity.[143]

        (1) Some thirty years after the resurrection, Paul cited the fact that more than five hundred people saw Jesus alive, and he says in effect, "If you do not believe me, you can ask them."[144]

        (2) Consider that women were the first witnesses of Christ's resurrection. Because women were not considered reliable witnesses in Jewish culture, had the church concocted the resurrection accounts to advance their own agenda, they doubtless would not have written women witnesses into the narrative.[145]

        (3) Christ appeared to the disciples on at least ten occasions.

    d. UUs give no reason for rejecting the miraculous occurrences involving Jesus, other than that they offend their "scientific" sensibilities.

  4. Unlike the teachings of any other human being, Jesus' teachings are infallible and possess absolute, final authority.

    a. Jesus himself claimed that his teachings have final authority.

        (1) Matthew 7:24–29—Unlike the Pharisees, Jesus and his teaching possess authority.

        (2) Matthew 24:35—Heaven and earth will pass away, but Jesus' words stand sure.

        (3) Matthew 28:18—"Then Jesus came to them and said, 'All authority in heaven and on earth has been given to me.'"

        (4) See also Matthew 9:6; Mark 1:27; 2:10; Luke 4:32, 36; 5:24; John 5:27; 10:7–9; 12:48; Revelation 2:27; 12:10.

    b. Jesus' apostles taught that Jesus' teachings have final authority.

        (1) Acts 4:12—"There is no other name under heaven given to men by which we must be saved."

        (2) Romans 2:16—Paul taught that "God will judge men's secrets through Jesus Christ, as my gospel declares."

        (3) 1 Thessalonians 4:2—Paul gave instructions on the authority of the Lord Jesus.

        (4) 1 Timothy 6:3–5—Paul declared that anyone who teaches contrary to what the Lord Jesus taught is a false teacher.

---

[143]On the authenticity of resurrection accounts, see Craig, "Did Jesus Rise from the Dead?" 141–76. See also Colin Brown, *That You May Believe* (Grand Rapids: Eerdmans, 1985); *Miracles and the Critical Mind* (Grand Rapids: Eerdmans; Exeter, Devon: Paternoster, 1984); C. S. Lewis, *Miracles: A Preliminary Study* (New York, Macmillan, 1947); Richard Swinburne, ed., *Miracles* (New York: Macmillan, 1989); and R. Douglas Geivett and Gary Habermas, *In Defense of Miracles: A Comprehensive Case for God's Action in History* (Downers Grove, Ill.: InterVarsity Press, 1997).

[144]See Yamauchi, quoting D. E. Nineham, in "Easter—Myth, Hallucination, or History?" (Part 2 of 2), *Christianity Today*, 29 March 1974, 14.

[145]Ibid.; and Craig, "Did Jesus Rise from the Dead?" 154.

    c. If Jesus' teachings were fallible while he claimed them to be infallible, then Jesus was a liar or was deluded.

  5. Jesus Christ was much more than simply a great ethical teacher.

    a. Christians disagree that this is *all* Jesus was.

    b. The phrase "great ethical teacher" is ambiguous, since it can mean that Jesus was a great teacher who was personally ethical or that he taught a system of ethics that was great.

    c. In either sense of the phrase, UUs are inconsistent in revering Jesus as a great ethical teacher while at the same time denying the truth of certain claims that Jesus made for himself. Jesus both claimed to be the final religious authority (see point 4 above) and based his ethical teachings on truths denied by UUs, such as that salvation comes only through faith in him (John 6:28–29, 40).

    d. C. S. Lewis sums up the matter cogently:

> "A man who was merely a man and said the sort of things Jesus said would not be a great moral teacher. He would either be a lunatic—on the level with the man who says he is a poached egg—or else he would be the Devil of Hell. You must make your choice. Either this man was, and is, the son of God: or else a madman or something worse."[146]

D. The Biblical View of Jesus Christ

  1. Jesus Christ is fully God.

    a. Isaiah 9:6—This passage, which obviously is Messianic, calls Jesus "the Mighty God."

    b. John 1:1, 14—"The Word was God. . . . The Word became flesh and made his dwelling among us."

      (1) The beginning of verse 14 shows that it refers to Jesus and is an obvious reference to his incarnation.

      (2) Yet, this same Word is also called "God" in verse 1.

      (3) Verse 1 fits a Trinitarian, not a Unitarian, perspective. The same Word who is *with* God (i.e., the Father) is also himself God (i.e., God the Son).[147]

    c. John 1:3—Jesus is the uncreated creator, hence he must be God.

    d. John 1:18—Jesus is called "God the One and Only [Greek, *monogenes*], who is at the Father's side"—*monogenes* meaning "unique; one of a kind."[148]

    e. John 8:24, 58 (KJV, NASB)—Harkening back to Exodus 3:14, Jesus applies the divine name ("I AM") to himself.[149]

---

[146]C. S. Lewis, *Mere Christianity* (New York: Macmillan, 1960), 40–41.

[147]On this text, see Bowman, *Jehovah's Witnesses*, 24–25; Murray Harris, *Jesus as God* (Grand Rapids: Baker, 1992), 51–71; and Grudem, *Systematic Theology*, 233–35, esp. 234 n.12.

[148]See footnote 139 above.

[149]See Grudem, *Systematic Theology*, 169. The NIV's rendering of verse 24 should be rejected.

    f. John 20:28—Thomas calls Jesus "God," and Jesus receives the title and Thomas's worship, pronouncing Thomas "blessed."

    g. Romans 9:5—Paul calls Jesus "God over all."[150]

    h. Titus 2:13; 2 Peter 1:1—Our savior Jesus is also called "God."[151]

    i. Hebrews 1:3–4, 8—The writer to the Hebrews declares that Jesus is the exact representation of God's being.[152] In verse 8 the writer explicitly calls the son "God."

2. Jesus Christ is fully man.

    a. The Bible explicitly affirms Jesus' humanity.

      (1) 1 Timothy 2:5—"For there is one God and one mediator between God and men, the man Christ Jesus."

      (2) John 1:1, 14; 1 John 4:2; 2 John 7—These passages, which talk about Jesus coming in the "flesh," refer to his humanity—his entire human nature, not just his body.

      (3) Hebrews 2:14—Jesus shares a common humanity with us.

      (4) 1 Corinthians 15:45—Christ is called the "last Adam." This shows his participation in the human race.

      (5) Matthew 1:1–17; Romans 1:3; 9:5—Jesus' human lineage.

    b. Jesus displayed attributes of humanity, showing true manhood.

      (1) Jesus had a body (Luke 24:39; John 1:1, 14; 6:51–56; Acts 2:31; Eph. 2:15; Rom. 1:3; 8:3; 1 John 4:2; 2 John 7; Heb. 10:5).

      (2) Jesus felt hunger (Luke 4:2).

      (3) Jesus grew, both physically and mentally (Luke 2:52).

      (4) Jesus experienced human temptations (Mark 1:13; Luke 4:1–2; 22:28; Heb. 2:18; 4:15).

V. The Doctrines of Man[153] and Sin

A. *Unitarian Universalist Positions on Man and Sin Briefly Stated*

1. UUs affirm the dignity and worth of all human beings.
2. UUs teach that human beings are the products of evolution.
3. UUs deny the doctrine of original sin—that is, people are not "born in sin."
4. UUs emphasize human ability to do good.

---

[150]As to why this verse applies the title "God" to Jesus and not to the Father, see R. C. H. Lenski, *The Interpretation of St. Paul's Epistle to the Romans* (Columbus, Ohio: Wartburg Press, 1945), 586–89.

[151]On the grammar of these passages see Grudem, *Systematic Theology,* 236 n.15; Harris, *Jesus as God,* 173–85; and E. Calvin Beisner, *"Jesus Only" Churches* (Grand Rapids: Zondervan, 1998), 46, in this series.

[152]Grudem, *Systematic Theology,* 236.

[153]*Man* is here intended in its wider generic sense. The phrase "doctrine of man" is so common in theological discourse that to invent a gender-inclusive substitute would likely cause confusion.

B. Arguments Used by Unitarian Universalists to Support Their Positions on Man and Sin

1. UUs affirm the dignity and worth of all human beings.

    a. The *Principles and Purposes* statement of the UUA espouses "the inherent worth and dignity of every person."[154]

    b. Duncan Howlett affirms, "Belief in the dignity and worth of every person is fundamental. It is an article of faith so basic there is nothing more basic to rest it on."[155]

    c. Rankin states, "We believe in the worth and dignity of each human being."[156]

2. UUs teach that human beings are the products of evolution.

    "[Question:] Do you believe in the concept of evolution? [Answer:] Yes."[157]

3. UUs deny the doctrine of original sin—that is, people are not "born in sin."

    a. UU minister Leonard Mason quips, "Come return to your place in the pews, and hear our heretical views: You were not born in sin so lift up your chin, you have only your dogmas to lose."[158]

    b. "Unitarian Universalists reject the traditional Christian idea that the original sin of disobedience of Adam is inherited by all and can only be eliminated by God's 'grace' operating through the church."[159]

    c. "You could attend a UU church for years and seldom hear the word sin."[160]

4. UUs emphasize human ability to do good.

    a. "Rather than feel bound by human weaknesses and frailties, we emphasize human strengths. We believe people have the strength, power and intelligence to make good things happen. You might call it a 'can do' religion."[161]

    b. "Unitarian Universalism believes in 'salvation by character,' that is, we are capable of achieving more ideal lives as the result of our own efforts to strengthen and sensitize ourselves. It does not rely on some supernatural intervention."[162]

    c. "Our moral fiber is equal to all demands."[163]

---

[154]*UUA 1997–98 Directory*, 3.

[155]Duncan Howlett, quoted in Strong, *Can I Believe Anything I Want?*

[156]Rankin, *What Do Unitarian Universalists Believe?* point 6.

[157]Sias, *100 Questions*, 4. On the historical importance of Darwinism to UU belief, see Parke, "Theological Directions," 11.

[158]Sias, *100 Questions*, 1.

[159]Chworowsky and Raible, "What Is a Unitarian Universalist?" 267–68.

[160]Sias, *100 Questions*, 9–10.

[161]Ibid., 13.

[162]Marshall, *Challenge of a Liberal Faith*, 31.

[163]Ibid., 47.

C. Refutation of Arguments Used by Unitarian Universalists to Support Their Positions on Man and Sin

1. Human beings do have dignity and worth, which is why Unitarian Universalism is to be rejected.

   a. Evolution greatly devalues the actual worth of human beings, who are created in God's image.[164] (See discussion at V.D.1 below.)

   b. As a group, UUs are also pro-abortion,[165] which devalues human worth.[166]

   c. Human beings are not of "supreme worth," contra Marshall's claim.

      (1) Only God is of "supreme" worth (Isa. 42:8; 46:5; Matt. 4:10; 22:37–40; Rom. 1:18–32; 11:36).

      (2) God's creation has worth in so far as it reflects God's workmanship. Though men and women are of tremendous worth, their worth in no way approaches that of their creator.

      (3) To ascribe supreme worth to anything but God is idolatry, which God condemns (1 Cor. 6:9; Rev. 21:8; 22:15).

   d. It is simply not true that "no idea, ideal, or philosophy is superior to a single human life."

      (1) Rankin's statement is somewhat obscure, but presumably he means that there is no idea worth dying for.

      (2) If Rankin is correct, why do UUs often hold up Unitarian martyrs (e.g.; Servetus) as objects of admiration? If ideas are not worth dying for, these people ought not to be admired but scorned, since they could have denied their ideals and saved "a single human life" (i.e., their own).

      (3) If Jesus Christ had held to Rankin's maxim, he would not have acted on his ideals and would not have given his life "a ransom for many" (Matt. 20:28; see also Rom. 5:8).

2. Human beings, since the fall of Adam and Eve, are "born in sin." That is, the biblical doctrine of original sin is true.

   a. The term *original sin* includes two elements: our judicial guilt before God (Gen. 3:6; Rom. 5:12, 16–19), and the corruption of our

---

[164]On the problems inherent in the theory of evolution, see J. P. Moreland, *The Creation Hypothesis* (Downers Grove, Ill.: InterVarsity Press, 1994); Philip E. Johnson, *Darwin on Trial* (Downers Grove, Ill.: InterVarsity Press, 1991); Charles B. Thaxton, Walter L. Bradley, and Roger L. Olsen, *The Mystery of Life's Origin: Reassessing Current Theories* (New York: Philosophical Library, 1984); and Michael J. Behe, *Darwin's Black Box: The Biochemical Challenge to Evolution* (New York: Free Press, 1996). For critiques of evolution by non-Christian scientists, see Hoimar V. Ditfurth, *The Origins of Life* (New York: Harper and Row, 1982); Michael Denton, *Evolution: A Theory in Crisis* (Bethesda: Adler and Adler, 1985); and Robert Shapiro, *Origins: A Skeptic's Guide to the Creation of Life on Earth* (New York: Bantam, 1986).

[165]See Part I, Section V.C.2 above.

[166]See Francis J. Beckwith, *Politically Correct Death: Answering Arguments for Abortion Rights* (Grand Rapids: Baker, 1993).

    natures—with a bias toward sin—that is passed down through natural generation.

    b. The Bible clearly teaches this doctrine. (See D.2 below.)

    c. Experience readily attests to the reality of original sin.

      (1) Sin's universality is evident through empirical observation. No one can point to a sinless person unless we redefine sin.[167]

      (2) Our own consciousness of sin comports with the doctrine, through observing the sinfulness of others and awareness of our own moral failings.

    d. Though infants cannot commit sinful acts (i.e., transgressions), they are nonetheless sinful *by nature,* as any parent can attest.

  3. Because of their sinfulness, human beings are limited in their ability to do good. (See discussion of total depravity at D.4 below.)

D. The Biblical Doctrines of Man and Sin

  1. Human beings are created in God's image.

    a. See Genesis 1:26–27; also Genesis 5:1; 9:6; 1 Corinthians 11:7; James 3:9.

    b. Grudem asserts that "every way in which man is like God is part of his being in the image and likeness of God."[168]

    c. The image of God in man entails a rational, moral, spiritual, and social likeness and may also include the notion of dominion over the earth. It does not include a bodily resemblance, since God is spirit (Luke 24:39; John 4:24).

    d. Man is not divine (see IV.C.1 above). Image is not to be equated with deity.

  2. Human beings fell through Adam's transgression.

    a. As mentioned above, original sin includes both judicial guilt and a corruption of our natures (Jer. 17:9; Matt. 7:11; Rom. 7:18; Eph. 2:1–3; 1 John 1:8); this corruption is inherited (Job 14:4; 15:14; 25:4; Ps. 51:5; Rom. 5:19).

    b. Romans 5:15–21 teaches that the human race is judicially liable for Adam's sin.

  3. Sin is any lack of conformity to God's character.

    a. Several Greek and Hebrew words are translated by the single word "sin," emphasizing different aspects of failing to meet God's holy standard (1 John 3:4).

---

[167]For example, one may minimize moral failings as "mistakes," "weaknesses," or "imperfections," denying that they are sin. Nevertheless, these are sins, regardless of attempts to rationalize them away.

[168]Grudem, *Systematic Theology,* 444.

  b. The most common Greek word is *hamartia,* which means "every departure from the way of righteousness, both human and divine"[169] (see Romans 3:23).

  c. People fall short by failing to do what they should (James 4:17) and by doing what they should not (1 John 3:4).

  d. Sin includes both *actions* and *attitudes* (e.g., anger: Matt. 5:22; covetousness: Ex. 20:17; lust: Matt. 5:28; jealousy: Gal. 5:20).

4. Human beings are "totally depraved."

  a. "Total depravity" means that sin taints all aspects of who and what we are. It does not mean that people are as sinful as they can possibly be.

  b. Grudem notes, "It is not just that some parts of us are sinful and others are pure. Rather, every part of our being is affected by sin—our intellects, our emotions and desires, our hearts (the center of our desires and decision-making processes), our goals and motives, and even our physical bodies."[170]

  c. The Bible indicates that, since the Fall, sin pervades the soul.

   (1) Romans 7:18—"I know that nothing good lives in me, that is, in my sinful nature."

   (2) Jeremiah 17:9—"The heart is deceitful above all things and beyond cure. Who can understand it?"

   (3) Ephesians 4:18—Unbelievers are "darkened in their understanding and separated from the life of God because of the ignorance that is in them due to the hardening of their hearts."

  d. Because people are totally depraved, they cannot do any spiritual good before God apart from his grace in salvation.

   (1) People can do good acts, but not with the motive of bringing glory to God.

   (2) Isaiah 64:6—"All our righteous acts are like filthy rags."

   (3) John 15:5—On bearing a fruitful life of good works pleasing to God, Jesus said, "Apart from me you can do nothing."

   (4) Philippians 2:13—Christians can do spiritually good works through God's power in their lives; "it is God who works in [them] to will and to act according to his good purpose."

5. Death is the punishment for sin.

  a. The essence of "death" is separation.

   (1) Physical death is the separation of the soul from the body.

   (2) Spiritual death is the separation of the person from God.

---

[169]*BAG,* s.v. *"hamartia."*
[170]Grudem, *Systematic Theology,* 497.

  b. The Bible speaks of death in general as the punishment for sin (Gen. 2:17; Ezek. 18:4, 20; Rom. 5:12).[171]

  c. Other passages focus on spiritual death—separation from God.[172]

   (1) Ephesians 2:1—People are spiritually "dead" before salvation. This refers to their alienation from God in this present life.

   (2) Revelation 2:11; 20:6; 21:8—The "second death" is eternal separation from God in the lake of fire.

   (3) Matthew 7:23; 8:12; Luke 13:25–27; 2 Thessalonians 1:8–9 emphasize banishment (eternal separation) from God's presence.

 6. Salvation from sin is both necessary and possible. (See VI.D below.)

VI. The Doctrine of Salvation

A. Unitarian Universalist Positions on Salvation Briefly Stated

 1. All people are children of God.

 2. UUs reject "salvation" from sin in the traditional Christian sense.

 3. When UUs speak of Jesus as a "savior," they do so loosely.

 4. It is arrogant and narrow-minded to say that Jesus is the only way of salvation.

 5. "Salvation" consists in making this present world a better place.

 6. Because humans are capable of virtuous living, they do not need "grace" but can "save" themselves through their moral character.

B. Arguments Used by Unitarian Universalists to Support their Positions on Salvation

 1. All people are children of God.

  a. "The [UU] theist, recognizing one God, and 'one light that lighteth every man and woman that comes into the world,' has no choice but to acknowledge all men and women as children of God; the atheist as well as the orthodox, the sinner as well as the saint."[173]

  b. "This modern faith asserts the goodness of all; it sees each as the child of God or, as many of us would say, as the child of the universe."[174]

  c. Robert Fulghum, UU minister and best-selling author, states, "God is immanent. God is at all places at all times. We're all sons of God."[175]

---

[171]These passages certainly have at least physical death in view, and possibly also include spiritual death.

[172]The doctrine of eternal punishment is treated in VII.D below.

[173]Barbara W. Merritt, *The Faith of a Theist* (Boston: Unitarian Universalist Association, 1994).

[174]Marshall, *Challenge of a Liberal Faith,* 31.

[175]Religious News Service, "'Kindergarten' Writer Says Point Was Missed," *Los Angeles Times,* 21 December 1991, Orange County Edition, S-7.

2. UUs reject "salvation" in the traditional Christian sense.

    a. "Unitarian Universalism is not a salvation religion."[176]

    b. "Since we believe in neither original sin nor hell, we do not feel a need to be saved from either."[177]

    c. "Unitarian Universalists reject the idea that God sacrificed Jesus 'His Son' to 'atone' for human 'sin.'"[178]

3. When UUs speak of Jesus as a "savior," they do so loosely.

    a. "We respect religious and spiritual leaders such as Jesus, Moses and Buddha for what they can teach us about living, not as redeemers in the traditional sense."[179]

    b. "The world has many saviors and I revere all who have tried to help their fellow man and woman."[180]

4. It is arrogant and narrow-minded to say that Jesus is the only way of salvation.

    a. Tony Larsen urges UUs to respond to "narrow-minded Christians" as follows:

    "Question: What can you say if someone asks you if you believe in Christ as your Savior? *Answer:* I can say, 'I believe that Jesus lived and taught things that are valuable for living, but I also believe that many others have too, so the world has many saviors and I revere all who have tried to help their fellow man and woman.'"[181]

    b. Harry Hoehler, who considers himself a UU Christian, argues against the exclusivity of Christ as savior.[182]

5. "Salvation" consists of making this present world a better place.

    a. Charles A. Gaines, director of the UUA Department of Extension, says, "We need more people thinking about saving our environment, guaranteeing individual free choice, promoting justice and compassion.... We need more people speaking our values and voting for the persons who will translate Unitarian Universalist principles into concrete proposals for a better world. All this is what might be meant by the word 'salvation.'"[183]

---

[176]George N. Marshall, "Unitarian Universalism," in *Encounters with Eternity: Religious Views of Death and Life After-Death*, ed. C. J. Johnson and M. G. McGee (New York: Philosophical Library, 1986), 302.

[177]Sias, *100 Questions*, 10; see also 21.

[178]Chworowsky and Raible, "What Is a Unitarian Universalist?" 267–68. See also Marshall, *Challenge of a Liberal Faith*, 229.

[179]Sias, *100 Questions*, 10.

[180]Larsen, "Evangelizing Our Children," in *Salted with Fire*, 128.

[181]Ibid.

[182]Harry H. Hoehler, "Interfaith Dialogue: A Christian Perspective," *Unitarian Universalist Christian* 40, nos. 3–4 (Fall/Winter 1985): 39.

[183]Charles A. Gaines, "Counting the Ways to 250,000 by 2001," in *Salted with Fire*, 101.

    b. UU President Buehrens states, "The chief religious question is not 'What must I do to be saved?' but rather, 'What must we all do to save God's creation?'"[184]

6. Because human beings are capable of virtuous living, they do not need "grace" but can "save" themselves through their moral character.

    a. "Unitarian Universalism believes in 'salvation by character,' that is, we are capable of achieving more ideal lives as the result of our own efforts to strengthen and sensitize ourselves. It does not rely on some supernatural intervention."[185]

    b. "Our moral fiber is equal to all demands."[186]

C. Refutation of Arguments Used by Unitarian Universalists to Support Their Positions on Salvation

1. Not all people are God's children.

    a. All people are God's creatures and owe their existence to him (Ps. 100:3; Heb. 1:3), but God does not relate to everyone as "father" in terms of his eternal, spiritual family.

    b. We are adopted to be God's sons and daughters through faith (Rom. 8:15; Gal. 4:5; Eph. 1:5; see also John 1:12–13).

    c. These passages describe believers in Christ as God's children: Romans 8:14, 16; 9:8; Galatians 3:26; Ephesians 1:5; Hebrews 2:10, 13; 1 John 3:1–2, 10; Revelation 21:7.

    d. Scripture regards those who reject Christ as the devil's children, not God's (Matt. 23:15; John 8:44; 1 John 3:10).

2. The biblical doctrine of salvation is correct.

    a. Because the Bible is God's Word, what it teaches about salvation is true. (See II.D above.)

    b. UUs such as Chworowsky and Raible, who claim to be "inspired by the life and teachings of Jesus as an extraordinary fellow human being," would do well to be inspired by his extraordinary message of salvation.

    c. The biblical teaching about salvation is treated at point D below.

3. It is neither arrogant nor narrow-minded to teach that Jesus is the only way of salvation. (See I.C.3 above.)

4. Salvation does not consist in making this world a better place.

    a. Biblically speaking, salvation from sin entails being delivered from the judicial penalty and moral defilement of sin and being in God's blessed presence forever. (See point D below.)

    b. Because those who are truly Christ's manifest their salvation through a life of love and service to others (e.g., John 13:35; Eph.

---

[184]Buehrens, "Deeds Speak Louder," in *Salted with Fire,* 159.
[185]Marshall, *Challenge of a Liberal Faith,* 31; see also 124.
[186]Ibid., 47.

2:8–10), the world would be better if more people sought to live as his true disciples. But the UU view reverses the cause and effect; salvation could make the world better even though making a better world does not bring about salvation.[187]

5. People cannot save themselves through their own virtuous living.

    a. People do not have the ability to fulfill perfectly God's moral law (see V.D.4 above).

    b. Because people are unable to save themselves through human effort, he provides salvation as gift (Eph. 2:8–10; Gal. 2:16, 21). (See point D below.)

D. The Biblical Doctrine of Salvation

1. Salvation from sin is necessary to avoid eternal punishment.

    a. The Bible calls us (before salvation) dead in transgressions and sins (Eph. 2:1) and thus alienated from God (Col. 1:21) and in need of reconciliation (Rom. 5:10–11; 2 Cor. 5:18–20; Col. 1:20, 22).

    b. As God's enemies, we were objects of his wrath (John 3:36; Rom. 1:18; 2:5, 8; Eph. 2:3; 5:6; Col. 3:6; 1 Thess. 1:10; 2:16).

    c. Because all people continually fall short of God's perfect standard (Rom. 3:23; 1 John 1:8, 10), salvation from sin is needed to escape God's ultimate judgment.

2. Jesus Christ is the only Savior.[188]

    a. John 14:6—"Jesus answered, 'I am the way and the truth and the life. No one comes to the Father except through me.'"

    b. Acts 4:12—"Salvation is found in no one else, for there is no other name under heaven given to men by which we must be saved."

3. Jesus saves from sin through his work on the cross.

    a. Through his death, Christ provided all that is necessary to satisfy God's wrath against sin, resulting in our reconciliation with God through faith (Rom. 5:10; Col. 1:21–22).

    b. 1 John 2:2; Romans 3:25—John describes Jesus as the "propitiation" for our sins—the *hilasmos*, that which turns away, satisfies, or assuages wrath.[189]

    c. Scripture describes Christ's death as a ransom price—that is, liberation from sin's bondage (Matt. 20:28; Mark 10:45; Rom. 3:24; 1 Cor. 1:30; Gal. 4:5; Eph. 1:7; Col. 1:14; 1 Tim. 2:6; Heb. 9:12, 15).[190]

---

[187]C. S. Lewis makes this point cogently in his *Beyond Personality: The Christian Idea of God* (London: Centenary Press, 1944), 11.

[188]On this subject, see Ronald H. Nash, *Is Jesus the Only Savior?* (Grand Rapids: Zondervan, 1994).

[189]Leon Morris, *The Apostolic Preaching of the Cross* (Grand Rapids: Eerdmans, 1965), 178; George Smeaton, *The Apostles' Doctrine of the Atonement* (Grand Rapids: Zondervan, 1957), 455; Charles Hodge, *Systematic Theology*, 3 vols. (Grand Rapids: Eerdmans, 1979), 2:508–9.

[190]Morris, *The Apostolic Preaching of the Cross*, 12, 48, 61; Liddell and Scott, *An Intermediate Greek-English Lexicon* (Oxford: Clarendon, 1975), 481.

4. Christ's work is appropriated solely and simply through faith in Christ.

a. The Bible makes it clear that we are saved through faith in Christ (e.g., Acts 16:31; Rom. 10:9–10; 1 Cor. 1:21; Eph. 2:8–10).

b. The Bible says we are *justified* by faith (Acts 13:39; Rom. 3:26, 30; 4:5; 5:1; 10:10; Gal. 2:16; 3:8, 11, 24)—that is, declared "not guilty" before the bar of God's justice.[191]

c. God is able to declare us "not guilty" because Christ's righteousness is imputed to us ("credited to our accounts") through our faith in his atoning work (Rom. 3:21–2; 4:3–11, 22–25; Gal. 3:6).

d. Biblical faith is essentially *trust*. Grudem states, "Saving faith is trust in Jesus Christ as a living person for forgiveness of sins and for eternal life with God."[192]

5. The one who is saved possesses eternal life as God's gift.

a. Because salvation is received by faith alone, it follows that salvation is God's free gift.

b. To be saved, one need simply believe; no other conditions must be met (Acts 2:37–38;[193] 16:31; Rom. 10:9; Eph. 2:8–9).

c. As a gift, salvation cannot be earned through performing good works (Rom. 3:20, 23–24; Gal. 2:16; 3:11; 5:4; Titus 3:7).

d. When we are saved we have peace with God (Rom. 5:1; Col. 1:20) and eternal life (e.g., Matt. 25:46; John 3:15–16, 36; 5:21, 24; 6:40, 47; 10:28; 12:25; 17:2–3; Acts 13:48; Rom. 5:21; 6:22–23).

VII. The Doctrines of Heaven, Hell, and the Afterlife

A. *Unitarian Universalist Positions on Heaven, Hell, and the Afterlife Briefly Stated*

1. Probably most UUs deny the existence of an afterlife, including a literal heaven or hell.

2. Some UUs are agnostic about the existence of an afterlife, while others do believe in it or at least feel that the evidence points in that direction.[194]

4. UUs focus their attention on this present life, not on some hypothetical life in an age to come.

5. Whatever their view of an afterlife, UUs deny the bodily resurrection.

6. A God of love would never send anyone to hell, if such a place did exist.

---

[191]Grudem, *Systematic Theology*, 723; *BAG*, s.v. *"dikaioo."*

[192]Grudem, *Systematic Theology*, 710.

[193]Repentance should not be seen as separate from faith but as part of it. Repentance is a description of the faith process seen from the standpoint of moving away from unbelief to belief in Christ. This change of mind—from not trusting in Christ to trusting in him—is repentance.

[194]Church, "Awakening," in *Our Chosen Faith*, 15–16.

73

7. There is no future judgment; people are compensated in this life for what they do.

B. *Arguments Used by Unitarian Universalists to Support Their Positions on Heaven, Hell, and the Afterlife*

1. Probably most UUs deny the existence of an afterlife, including a literal heaven or hell.

   a. According to a 1989 survey, only 15 percent believe in life after death, 46 percent do not, and 38 percent are not sure.[195]

   b. Edington states, "Most UUs regard death as the final and total end of our existence."[196]

2. Some UUs are agnostic about the existence of an afterlife.

   a. UU "Christian" Thomas Wintle states, "I don't know what happens to us after we die, whether there is nothing or there is light"[197]

   b. Marshall sums up UU agnosticism on the afterlife: "We simply do not know, and we question scriptural passages that seem to say otherwise."[198]

   c. Ada Barnett Stough weighs several ideas, including cessation, some kind of cosmic milieu, or Eastern reincarnation.[199]

3. Some UUs do believe in an afterlife, or at least feel that the evidence points in that direction.

   Robert Slater believes that "laboratory evidence gathered by parapsychologists" suggests that "the real and essential part of us does indeed survive the death of the body."[200]

4. UUs focus their attention on this present life, not on some hypothetical life in an age to come.

   a. "This faith accepts a scientific view of life and sees life as lived in the here and now rather than in the hereafter."[201]

   b. "There is enough hell in this world without creating an imaginary hell in another world."[202]

5. Whatever their view of an afterlife, UUs deny the bodily resurrection.

   a. Chworowsky and Raible state, "Unitarian Universalists emphatically reject [the virgin birth and bodily resurrection] as contrary to both scientific and historical evidence."[203]

---

[195]UUA, *The Quality of Religious Life in Unitarian Universalist Congregations,* 46. See also Marshall, *Challenge of a Liberal Faith,* 217–18.

[196]Sias, *100 Questions,* 4, 9.

[197]Jane Rzepka, ed., *Death and Immortality: Unitarian Universalist Views* (Boston: Unitarian Universalist Association, 1994), 5.

[198]Marshall, "Unitarian Universalism," 300. See also Johnson and McGee, *Encounters with Eternity,* Appendix, 325, 327.

[199]Ada Barnett Stough, cited in Larsen and Schmidt, *Catechism,* 13–14.

[200]Rzepka, *Death and Immortality,* 9.

[201]Johnson and McGee, *Encounters with Eternity,* Appendix, 325, 327.

[202]Marshall, *Challenge of a Liberal Faith,* 231; see also 237.

[203]Chworowsky and Raible, "What Is a Unitarian Universalist?" 267.

b. "Because bodily decay occurs rapidly following death, from the scientific point of view, bodily resurrection is not possible. The spirit may continue somehow or in some form."[204]

6. A God of love would never send anyone to hell, if such a place did exist.

   a. "What happens at the end of time and/or at a Judgment Day? ... No one knows, but a loving God would not condemn any person to eternal damnation."[205]

   b. Schulz quips, "If you hear someone preaching hellfire and damnation or that the future is solely in the hands of God, chances are it's not a Unitarian Universalist!"[206]

   c. Larsen states, "When it comes to a god who would condemn souls to hell, I'm an atheist. I can't believe in that kind of deity."[207]

7. There is no future judgment; people are compensated in this life for what they do.

   a. "We believe that human beings should be accountable for their actions and make amends for any harm they may bring to others. But we don't believe that God will punish them."[208]

   b. "No one 'goes' to hell; people create their own hells here on earth.... As with the good, what evil people do is compensated for in this life. 'Compensation' is the U.U. position."[209]

C. *Refutation of Arguments Used by Unitarian Universalists to Support Their Positions on Heaven, Hell, and the Afterlife*

1. UUs are wrong to deny the existence of an afterlife or even to be agnostic about it.

   a. The UUs' dogmatic agnosticism about the afterlife is self-refuting.

      (1) As noted above, some UUs are not content to say simply that *they* do not know whether there is an afterlife; they affirm dogmatically that *no one knows anything about it*.

      (2) To say that *no one* can know anything about the afterlife, there must be at least *something* that *can* be known about the afterlife, namely, its unknowability.

      (3) Thus this dogmatic form of agnosticism entails a patent contradiction. A more reasonable form of agnosticism would not deny the possibility of knowing whether there is an afterlife simply because UUs themselves are unsure.

---

[204]Johnson and McGee, *Encounters with Eternity*, Appendix, 338, 340. See also Marshall, "Unitarian Universalism," 301.

[205]Johnson and McGee, *Encounters with Eternity*, Appendix, 335, 338.

[206]Schulz, "Our Faith," 3.

[207]Larsen and Schmidt, *Catechism*, 5.

[208]Sias, *100 Questions*, 13.

[209]Johnson and McGee, *Encounters with Eternity*, Appendix, 331, 333, 335.

   b. We have it on no less than the authority of the Son of God that
there is an afterlife.

     (1) In numerous passages Jesus affirmed that there is life after
death.

     (2) Jesus taught that those who believe in him will experience
eternal life in heaven (e.g., Matt. 5:12; 6:20; 8:11; 18:3–4;
19:21, 23, 29; 25:46; Mark 10:21, 30; Luke 6:23; 16:9; 18:30).

     (3) Jesus taught that those who reject him will have unending
existence, but banished from his presence (e.g., Matt. 5:22, 30;
10:28; 23:33; 25:41, 46; Mark 9:43, 45, 47; Luke 12:5).

   c. Christ's apostles also taught that there is life after death.

     (1) Many passages declare that believers have "eternal life" (John
3:15–16, 36; 17:2–3; Acts 13:48; Rom. 5:21; 6:22–23; 1 Tim.
6:12; Titus 1:2; 3:7; 1 John 1:2; 2:25; 5:11–13; Jude 21).

     (2) Paul acknowledged that when he departed this life he would be
present with the Lord (2 Cor. 5:8; Phil. 1:23; 2 Tim. 4:8).

     (3) Wintle's use of 1 Corinthians 2:9 to suggest that Paul was
unclear about the existence of the afterlife is a gross misinter-
pretation of that text.[210] It is refuted simply by reading verse 10.

   d. People *have* returned from the dead, offering empirical proof that
there is life after death.

     (1) Marshall's statement, "No one has ever returned to tell us
about the afterlife," is simply false.

     (2) Jesus came back from the dead and presented himself alive
before many witnesses (Acts 1:3; 1 Cor. 15:4–8).

     (3) Before Christ arose, some believers came back from the dead,
such as Lazarus (John 11:44) and certain saints who were
raised while Jesus was dead (Matt. 27:52).[211]

2. While true Christians seek to make this world a better place, nevertheless they look forward to life in the age to come.

   a. Christians, ancient and modern, have taken life in this world seriously.

   b. It does not follow that because Christians anticipate a better age
to come, they are indifferent about this present one.

     (1) Christians have engaged in various and many works of charity,
have fought against injustice, and even risked their lives to
hide Jews from the Nazis.[212]

---

[210]See Jane Rzepka, *Death and Immortality*, 5.

[211]Note that these cases are really more resuscitations than resurrections, since the individuals eventually died again. Nonetheless, these individuals did truly return from the grave to life.

[212]Consider the example of Corrie ten Boom, *The Hiding Place*, with John and Elizabeth Sherrill (Washington Depot, Conn.: Chosen Books, 1971).

    (2) Paul said that Christians are to do good to all people (Gal. 6:10).

  c. It is precisely *because* God has given us eternal life that Christians show their thankfulness for his great gift by doing good in this life.

  d. UUs know that Christian beliefs motivate people to action in this life, otherwise they would not view the so-called Religious Right with such alarm.

3. The bodily resurrection is to be believed.

  a. Jesus taught that he would rise from the dead (Matt. 16:21; 17:23; 20:19; Mark 10:34; Luke 9:22; John 2:19; 10:17), as would others (Matt. 22:30; John 5:21, 25–26, 29; 6:40, 54; 11:24).

  b. Jesus' apostles taught the resurrection from the dead (e.g., Acts 1:22; 2:24, 30–32; Rom. 1:4; 4:24–25; 6:4–5, 9; 1 Cor. 6:14; 15; 1 Peter 1:3, 21; 3:21; Rev. 20:5, 6).

  c. The UU rejection of the bodily resurrection as "unscientific" is both arbitrary and begs the question.

    (1) It is mere dogmatic prejudice to say that a resurrection cannot occur simply because no modern scientist has witnessed one.

    (2) To reject the bodily resurrection as unscientific because dead bodies decompose when left in their natural state is to beg the question. The whole point of the resurrection is that it will involve a *supernatural* act of God, in which he will reconstitute the body that is sown in the ground, revivify it, and raise it to a glorious state (1 Cor. 15:35–37, 44).

    (3) Paul refuted those who rejected the bodily resurrection on "scientific" grounds, calling them "fools" (1 Cor. 15:36).

  d. Christ's bodily resurrection was a well-attested historical event.

    (1) Many solid, scholarly works argue for this historicity.[213]

    (2) The UU rejection of the resurrection as nonhistorical proceeds on dogmatic grounds, not based on an examination of the evidence.

4. God will punish the wicked in hell.

  a. The UU claim that a God of love would not send people to hell is false.

    (1) Although God is love (1 John 4:8, 16), he is also a righteous judge (Rom. 2:5; 2 Thess. 1:5–6; Rev. 16:7) and therefore must punish sin. If people are unwilling to have their sins paid for them by a substitute (2 Cor. 5:21), they must pay for them themselves.

    (2) Jesus had much to say about hell, as in Matthew 25:41.

---

[213]See the discussion at IV.C.3 above.

(3) The essence of hell is separation from God (Matt. 25:41; 2 Thess. 1:9).[214]

b. Contrary to the UU position, compensation does not always take place in this life.

(1) It is a fact both of Scripture and of experience that the wicked sometimes prosper in this life (Ps. 73; Jer. 5:28; 12:1).

(2) If the UUs are correct in saying that any and all compensation for evil takes place in this life, then the scales of justice will never be balanced. To consider but one example, Adolf Hitler never received adequate compensation during his lifetime for murdering six million innocent Jews.

(3) The biblical teaching about final judgment provides a basis for the belief that true, equitable, and complete compensation will occur (Col. 3:25; Rev. 20:12). (See D.2 below.)

D. The Biblical Doctrines of Heaven, Hell, and the Afterlife[215]

1. People who die in this present age exist in an "intermediate state," awaiting the final judgment.

a. The meaning of the term *intermediate state*

(1) Between death and the resurrection that will take place at the final judgment, there is an intermediate period in which those who have died continue in a state of conscious existence.

(2) The intermediate state is a temporary mode of existence; in the final state, which comes later, all people will be reembodied.

(3) Although all experience conscious, unresurrected existence, the quality of the intermediate state differs between the wicked and the righteous.

b. The nature of the intermediate state for the wicked

(1) The wicked are kept in a temporary state of punishment until the Day of Judgment (2 Peter 2:9).

(2) Luke 16:23 indicates that the wicked are kept in *Hades*,[216] which is a place of conscious torment.

(3) Although *Hades* is a place of punishment, it is not to be confused with the final and permanent punishment, which will take place in the lake of fire, also known as *Gehenna*.

---

[214]Donald Guthrie observes, "When we penetrate below the language about Hell, the major impression is a sense of separation" (*New Testament Theology* [Downers Grove, Ill.: InterVarsity Press, 1981], 889–90).

[215]On issues treated in this section, see Alan W. Gomes, "Evangelicals and the Annihilation of Hell," *Christian Research Journal* 13–14 (Spring/Summer, 1991); W. G. T. Shedd, *The Doctrine of Endless Punishment* (1886; reprint, Minneapolis: Klock and Klock, 1980); and Harry Buis, *The Doctrine of Eternal Punishment* (Philadelphia: Presbyterian and Reformed, 1957).

[216]No small confusion occurs because the single word *hell* in English is used to translate several different words in the original biblical languages. Therefore, here I use the original language words (e.g., *hades*, *gehenna*) rather than the less precise word *hell*.

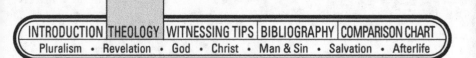
    c. The nature of the intermediate state for the righteous

       (1) When Christians die, they go immediately to be in the presence of the Lord (2 Cor. 5:8; Phil. 1:23).

       (2) Yet, during the intermediate state the righteous dead are also unresurrected. Unlike the wicked, however, they experience rest and peace in God's presence (Rev. 14:13).

  2. The final judgment follows the intermediate state. A person's final abode is determined at that time.

    a. The Bible is clear that there will be a final judgment for all mankind (Dan. 12:2; Matt. 10:15; 11:22, 24; 12:36; 25:41, 46; Luke 10:14; Acts 17:30–31; 24:25; Rom. 2:5; 14:10; 2 Cor. 5:10; Heb. 6:2; 9:27; 2 Peter 2:4, 9; 3:7; 1 John 4:17; Jude 6; Rev. 14:7; 20:11–15).

    b. The final judgment will not be overturned or contravened in any way.

       (1) Hebrews 9:27—"Man is destined to die once, and after that to face judgment."

       (2) Matthew 25:41, 46; Revelation 14:11; 20:10—Both the punishment of the wicked and the blessedness of the righteous are everlasting.

    c. Jesus Christ will be the judge (Matt. 25:31–33; John 5:26–27; Acts 10:42; 17:31; 2 Tim. 4:1).

    d. At the final judgment there will be a resurrection of the body, both for believers and for unbelievers. (See VII.C.3 above.)[217]

       (1) The wicked, thus removed from *Hades* and resurrected, will then be cast bodily into *Gehenna,* the lake of fire, for all eternity (Matt. 25:41; Mark 9:43, 47–48; Rev. 14:10–11; 20:14–15).[218]

       (2) The righteous will receive glorified bodies (Dan. 12:3; 1 Cor. 15:42–44) and experience eternal life with God in the new heaven and the new earth (Isa. 65:17; 66:22; 2 Peter 3:13; Rev. 21:1).

---

[217]See also the following Scripture passages: Dan. 12:2; Job 19:26–27; Matt. 22:30–31; Mark 12:25; Luke 14:14; 20:35–36; John 5:9; 6:39–40, 44, 54; 11:24–25; Acts 23:6; 24:15, 21; Rom. 6:5; 8:11; 1 Cor. 6:14; 15; 2 Cor. 4:14; Phil. 3:11; 1 Thess. 4:16; Heb. 6:2; Rev. 20:6.

[218]See Shedd, *Doctrine of Endless Punishment,* 46.

Part III:
Witnessing Tips

I. Understand the attraction of the UUA.

A. *Liberal Social Concerns*[1]

1. The UUA typically attracts upscale, college-educated liberals (both politically and religiously). If you can understand the attraction of liberalism generally, you will have a good sense of what attracts people to the UUA.

2. Liberals place (or purport to place) a high value on social issues, such as the environment, antidiscrimination, "economic justice," etc.; they hold to a "politically correct" ideology. Liberals fancy themselves as compassionate and caring, while they view conservatives (political and religious) as harsh, intolerant, and uncaring.

3. Although liberals themselves are arguably often far more intolerant than conservatives, you might wish to use their professed concern with "oppression" and "justice" as an opening for discussion.

   a. For example, you can show God's concern for treatment of the poor and downtrodden (e.g., as discussed throughout the book of Amos).

   b. You could then point out how Christians are concerned with alleviating the plight of the downtrodden, pointing to such examples as the Salvation Army, World Vision, and many other such groups.

B. *Antiauthoritarianism*

1. Another attraction to the UUA is a deeply-felt antiauthoritarianism. This is seen in a rebellion against absolute standards, whether creeds or Scripture itself.

2. Unitarian Universalism provides a person with an opportunity to be religious without having many moral restraints. UUs can experience the trappings of church—including the ceremony and sense of community—without having to submit to biblical morality commanded by an absolute God.

3. While this antiauthoritarianism will definitely pose a barrier, you must meet this issue head on. Nevertheless, do not fall into the trap of presenting the Christian faith as primarily a moral code or ethical system to which the UU must submit. This is to grant an error in UU thinking (see Part II, Section IV.C.5 above). Instead, stress that Christianity is a relationship with a person—the Lord Jesus Christ. Though

---

[1]For example, see Part I, Section V.C above.

this does involve submission to his commands (John 14:15, 23–24), be careful about how you present this. Following Christ's commandments is the *result* of a relationship with him, not its cause.

II. Treat each UU as an individual.

A. *The UUA is highly diverse—far more so than probably any other denomination.*

Consequently, when you meet someone who claims to be a UU, you should not presume to know his or her exact beliefs.

B. *Ask questions to determine the UU's beliefs.*

This is good practice in any evangelistic encounter, but it is especially critical here.

C. *Consider the worldview.*

Once you find out what kind of UU you are dealing with (e.g., a Neo-pagan, theist, nontheistic humanist, etc.), you may wish to learn about the worldview in question and look at the Christian response to it. For example, if you are talking to a Neo-pagan UU, you may wish to consult the volume in this series on witchcraft and Neo-paganism.

D. *Be prepared.*

You can be certain that whatever the UU *does* believe, he or she *will not* believe the essential doctrines of Christianity, so you should be prepared to discuss and defend these.

III. Be prepared to discuss the exclusive truth claims of the Christian faith.

A. *UUs eschew "exclusivism" and take offense at Christianity's exclusive truth claims.*

B. *Be prepared to confront this issue squarely.*

Study the arguments given in Part II, Section I.C.3 to explain why Christian "exclusivity" is not arrogant and unloving but is actually the most caring position possible.

C. *Be particularly careful about how you present this material.*

Do not fulfill the UU's stereotypical conception of a "fundamentalist" or member of the "radical Religious Right." Present them with the truth, but do so with a caring and compassionate attitude.

IV. Turn the argument around on them.

A. *The UU belief system comprises many patent contradictions.*

Yet UUs often prize themselves as committed to a rational, scientific approach to religion—in contrast to conservative Christianity, which they see as irrational and unthinking.

B. *Be prepared to respond to their criticisms in the following areas:*

1. When they say "all truth is relative," point out that this is an absolute statement. (See discussion at Part II, Section I.C.2.f.)

2. When they say "conservative Christians are religious bigots because they are exclusivistic," ask them if they are excluding your view. Point out this inconsistency. (See discussion at Part II, Section I.C.2.)

3. When they criticize Christian morals (e.g., rejection of homosexuality, abortion, premarital sex), ask them on what basis they can do this if truth is relative and if it is up to each individual to decide what is right for him or her. (See discussion at Part II, Section I.C.2.e.)

C. *You can also turn the tables on them by asking them questions.*

1. The UU will likely try to put you on the defensive by asking questions like, "Why are you Christians so narrow?" The UU, however, is not the only one entitled to ask questions; you should do the same.

2. Ask the UU questions like:

   a. "Why do you think there are many roads to God? What would lead you to conclude that?"

   b. "What reason do you have for thinking that all truth is relative?" (Then follow up by asking whether they think the truth of the reason they just gave is also relative.)

   c. "How do you justify thinking that you should trust your own moral intuitions above the morality that Jesus Christ taught?"

   d. "If you think Jesus was such a profound teacher, why do you dismiss out of hand so many of his teachings?"

3. Asking such questions may throw the UU off balance since it is quite likely that the UU has embraced his or her beliefs without much reflection.

4. After asking these questions, be prepared to show whatever weaknesses and fallacies appear in their answers.

Part IV: Selected Bibliography

Only a few of the most important sources are listed in the bibliography below. Consult also the footnotes throughout this book for additional relevant sources.

I. Sources on the Unitarian and Universalist History

Allen, J. H. *An Historical Sketch of the Unitarian Movement Since the Reformation.* New York: Christian Literature Co., 1894.

Wilbur, Earl Morse. *History of Unitarianism.* 2 vols. Vol. 1: Boston: Beacon Press, 1945. Vol. 2: Cambridge, Mass.: Harvard University Press, 1952. Reprint: Boston: Beacon Press, 1965.

These two volumes are the classic work on Unitarian history. Wilbur, himself a Unitarian, demonstrates an unsurpassed mastery of the primary historical documents. Though unparalleled in comprehensiveness, Wilbur's pro-Unitarian bias is evident throughout the book.

_____. *Our Unitarian Heritage.* Boston: Beacon Press, 1925.

Wright, Conrad, ed. *Three Prophets of Religious Liberalism: Channing, Emerson, Parker.* Boston: Beacon Press, 1961.

This reprint of three classic treatises by three important Unitarians provides important insights into nineteenth-century Unitarianism.

_____. *The Beginnings of Unitarianism in America.* Boston: Beacon Press, 1955.

II. Sources Published by UUs as General Surveys or Introductions to Their Beliefs and Practices

A. Pamphlets

The Unitarian Universalist Association publishes numerous pamphlets designed to acquaint inquirers with the beliefs and practices of Unitarian Universalism. Topics include views of God, Jesus, the Bible, homosexuality, and the church. Many of these pamphlets have been cited throughout this book. Refer to the footnotes for bibliographic information on these.

B. Books

Buehrens, John A. and F. Forrester Church. *Our Chosen Faith: An Introduction to Unitarian Universalism.* Boston: Beacon Press, 1989.

John Buehrens and F. Forrester Church coministered All Souls Church in Manhattan. Buehrens is now the UUA president. These prominent UU authors seek to present an overview of UU belief and practice, including why they chose Unitarian Universalism as their religious faith.

Chworowsky, Karl M. and Christopher Gist Raible. "What Is a Unitarian Universalist?" in *Religions in America,* edited by Leo Rosten (New York: Simon and Schuster, 1975), 263–76.

Leo Rosten's book presents an introduction to the beliefs of different religious groups. Chworowsky and Raible, a UU minister and a former Director of Extension for the UUA respectively, were selected to describe the key beliefs of the UUs. Their book provides clear, direct answers to key questions about God, sin, salvation, etc. However, because this was written in 1975, some answers may be dated. (I have cited them where their answers are in line with current UU thinking.)

Marshall, George N. *Challenge of a Liberal Faith.* Revised and Enlarged Edition. New Canaan, Conn.: Keats, 1980.

Author of at least seven books and numerous articles, Marshall has ministered in several UU congregations and retired as the minister and religious editor of the prominent UU Church of the Larger Fellowship. This book presents a good overview of UU beliefs, but is replete with fundamental historical blunders (e.g., Marshall places Thomas Aquinas "in the Counter Reformation, at the close of the medieval and the beginning of the modern era" [p. 18]; cites Zwingli as an anti-Trinitarian [pp. 130–31]; etc.).

_____. "Unitarian Universalism." In *Encounters with Eternity: Religious Views of Death and Life After Death,* edited by Christopher Jay Johnson and Marsha G. McGee. New York: Philosophical Library, 1986.

This book presents the views of different religious groups on death and the afterlife. Marshall presents the UU position(s). Marshall's chapter provides a clear presentation of UU belief, but it, too, contains historical errors, some egregious.

Schulz, William F. *The Unitarian Universalist Pocket Guide.* Second edition. Boston: Beacon Press, 1993.

Edited by the then-president of the UUA, this short book contains contributions from prominent UUs. It provides a concise overview of UU beliefs, practices, and social concerns. It also includes a handy chart listing important people and dates in Unitarian and Universalist history.

III. Other Writings of Interest by or About UUs

A. UU "Evangelism" and Propagating the UU Faith

Alexander, Scott W. *Salted with Fire.* Boston: Skinner House, 1995.

Edited by Scott Alexander, senior minister of the 2,000–member Church of the Larger Fellowship in Boston, this book illustrates well the shift that has taken place in the UUA—from a non- and even antiproselytizing group to one that has embarked on a militant program of expansion through "evangelism." This book sports contributions from leading denominational officials, including a foreword by past president William F. Schulz and a chapter by current president John A. Buehrens.

Chethik, Neil. "The Saving Message: The New UU Evangelists." *The World* 9, no. 3 (May-June 1995): 14–18.

Published in the UUA's own magazine, this article highlights recent UUA outreach activities.

Larsen, Tony and Ellen Schmidt. *A Catechism for Unitarian Universalists (Leader Guide)* Boston: Unitarian Universalist Association, 1989.

Larsen and Schmidt suggest nondogmatic ways to educate UUs about UU values and beliefs. The book contains exercises and thought-provoking questions that can be used in a small group or retreat setting. This book provides a fair survey of the pluralism in modern UUA belief.

B. Demographics, Statistics, and Items of General Reference

Kosmin, Barry A. and Lachman, Seymour P. *One Nation Under God.* New York: Harmony Books, 1993.

Kosmin and Lachman, researchers at the City University of New York, present the results of their survey of religious demographics. The largest and most comprehensive survey of its type, it shows that more than twice as many people consider themselves to be UUs than the official membership figures indicate. It also shows that UUs are the top religious group in measures of social status, education, and prestige.

Unitarian Universalist Association. *The Quality of Religious Life in Unitarian Universalist Congregations: A Survey by the Commission on Appraisal.* Boston: Unitarian Universalist Association, 1989.

Commissioned by the UUA, this study provides fascinating insights into contemporary UU attitudes and religious beliefs.

Unitarian Universalist Association. *Unitarian Universalist Association 1997–1998 Directory.* Boston: Unitarian Universalist Association, 1997.

Published annually, this directory provides important statistical information about the UUA, lists locations of congregations in the denomination, and discusses the various affiliate organizations found in the UUA.

C. Journal Articles on Humanism in the UUA

Kurtz, Paul and Vern L. Bullough. "The Unitarian Universalist Association: Humanism or Theism?" *Free Inquiry* 11, no. 2 (Spring 1991): 12–14.

McKown, Delos B. "A Humanist Looks at the Future of Unitarian Universalism." *Religious Humanism* 20, no. 2 (Spring 1986): 58–64, 70.

Olds, Mason. "Religious Humanism and Unitarianism." *Religious Humanism* 12, no. 1 (1978): 15–25.

This very insightful article gives an excellent history of humanism and its connection with the UUA.

D. Articles on "Christianity" and Christian-related Themes in the UUA

Gray, Duke T. "Letter to the Christians." *Unitarian Universalist Christian* 47, nos. 3–4 (Fall-Winter 1992): 40–52.

Gray, a UU "Christian," examines the contradictions and illogic involved in the UUA's pluralism. The article is important in that Gray is a UU, not an outside critic.

Hoehler, Harry H. "UUA Principles and Purposes: Is There a Place for UU Christians in the UUA? A Reply and Some Reflections." *Unitarian Universalist Christian* 38, nos. 3–4 (Fall-Winter 1983): 5–17.

Like Gray's article, Hoehler, a UU "Christian," discusses the theological schizophrenia inherent in the UUA's pluralism. Hoehler also cites what he feels is troubling evidence of hostility to liberal Christianity in the UUA. This article is noteworthy in that it is written by a UU, not a critic from the outside.

―――. "What It Means to be a Christian: A Unitarian Universalist Perspective." *Unitarian Universalist Christian* (Winter 1980–81).

Hoehler, Judith L. "The Bible as a Source of Feminist Theology." *Unitarian Universalist Christian* 37, nos. 3–4 (Fall-Winter 1982): 21–27.

Unlike many feminists who see the Bible as a patriarchal instrument of oppression, Judith Hoehler argues that key biblical themes, such as "liberation," can be helpfully appropriated by feminists in their quest for equality and freedom.

Straube, Arvid. "The Bible in Unitarian Universalist Theology." *Unitarian Universalist Christian* 44, no. 1 (1989): 22–29.

Trudinger, Paul. "St. Paul: A Unitarian Universalist Christian?" *Faith and Freedom* 43 (Spring-Summer 1990): 55–58.

Trudinger attempts (unsuccessfully) to argue that the apostle Paul held to a UU-like theology in many respects, including an alleged denial of the Trinity and of Christ's deity.

Unitarian Universalist Christian Fellowship (UUCF) Task Force. "Memoranda and Documents: Report of the UUCF Task Force on Mission (1976)." *Unitarian Universalist Christian* 47, nos. 3–4 (Fall-Winter 1992): 67–78.

This article documents the difficulties faced by liberal UU "Christians," stating, "We recognize that it has been increasingly difficult for Christians to continue to stay within Unitarian Universalism" (p. 67).

Part V:
Parallel Comparison Chart

Unitarian Universalism	The Bible
Divine Revelation and the Bible	
"THE TRUTH is not accessible to human grasp."[1]	"Jesus answered, 'I am the way and the truth and the life. No one comes to the Father except through me'" (John 14:6).
"We believe that personal experience, conscience and reason should be the final authorities in religion."[2]	"Trust in the LORD with all your heart and lean not on your own understanding" (Prov. 3:5).
"We carry our own light with us, and so we are never at a loss for our directions.... We do not rely upon external light."[3]	"Your word is a lamp to my feet and a light for my path" (Ps. 119:105). "Their minds and consciences are corrupted" (Titus 1:15).
"No one of the four Christs of the four gospels is the real Jesus through and through. Those Christs are theological concoctions made up in some part out of historical scraps of information about Jesus but in a greater part out of Christian faith and the polemical, apologetic, and idiosyncratic interests of each gospel writer. The frustrating, deplorable result of this, plus the everlasting paucity of the historical record, is that the real Jesus can never stand up to our inspection and questioning."[4]	"Therefore, since I myself have carefully investigated everything from the beginning, it seemed good also to me to write an orderly account for you, most excellent Theophilus, so that you may know the certainty of the things you have been taught" (Luke 1:3–4). "We are witnesses of everything he did in the country of the Jews and in Jerusalem" (Acts 10:39).

[1]Tom Owen-Towle, *Welcome to Unitarian Universalism: A Community of Truth, Service, Holiness and Love* (Boston: Unitarian Universalist Association, n.d.).

[2]Unitarian Universalist Association, *We Are Unitarian Universalists* (Boston: Unitarian Universalist Association, 1992).

[3]George N. Marshall, *Challenge of a Liberal Faith*, rev. and enl. ed. (New Canaan, Conn.: Keats Publishing, 1980), 45.

[4]Delos B. McKown, "A Humanist Looks at the Future of Unitarian Universalism," *Religious Humanism* 20, no. 2 (Spring 1986): 62–63.

"The Bible is, in its core and essence, a myth."[5] ". . . they [the biblical writers] used symbolic language, or 'mythology.'"[6]	"We did not follow cleverly invented stories [Greek *muthois*] when we told you about the power and coming of our Lord Jesus Christ, but we were eyewitnesses of his majesty" (2 Peter 1:16). (See also 2 Timothy 4:4.)

The Christian Faith

"It takes courage not to settle for a religion 'once for all delivered to the saints.'"[7] "The following of almost any religion can help a dedicated individual find a better and more meaningful life."[8]	"Earnestly contend for the faith which was once delivered unto the saints" (Jude 3). "There is a way that seems right to a man, but in the end it leads to death" (Prov. 14:12; 16:25). "Enter through the narrow gate. For wide is the gate and broad is the road that leads to destruction, and many enter through it" (Matt. 7:13).
"One thing, however, there is not: an ideology, a theological/religious faith stance, which our congregations have in common."[9]	"Do two walk together unless they have agreed to do so?" (Amos 3:3). "Do not be yoked together with unbelievers" (2 Cor. 6:14). (See also 1 Corinthians 1:10.)

---

[5]Arvid Straube, "The Bible in Unitarian Universalist Theology," *Unitarian Universalist Christian* 44, no. 1 (1989): 23.

[6]J. Frank Schulman, "An Affirmation that Life has Meaning," in *Unitarian Universalist Views of the Bible*, ed. Daniel G. Higgins, Jr. (Boston: Unitarian Universalist Association, 1994).

[7]Marshall, *Challenge of a Liberal Faith*, 18.

[8]Karl M. Chworowsky and Christopher Gist Raible, "What Is a Unitarian Universalist?" in *Religions in America*, ed. Leo Rosten (New York: Simon and Schuster, 1975), 272.

[9]Harry H. Hoehler, "Is There a Place for UU Christians in the UUA? A Reply and Some Reflections," *Unitarian Universalist Christian* 38, nos. 3–4 (Fall-Winter 1983): 6–7.

God

"People call God by many names. I call God, Jesus. I accept that you may have another name for god. Jesus is God to me."[10]

"In their [i.e., UU] churches are agnostics, humanists, even atheists—as well as nature worshippers, pantheists, and those who affirm a personal God."[11]

"... many Unitarian Universalists simply do not find a concept of God helpful to religious life."[12]

"Most of us do not believe in a supernatural, supreme being who can directly intervene in and alter human life or the mechanism of the natural world."[13]

"In general, Unitarian Universalists ... think of God as a unity rather than a trinity."[14]

"Paul was decidedly no trinitarian in the accepted traditional sense of the word. Special, Jesus was, but he was not God."[15]

"Then you call on the name of your god, and I will call on the name of the LORD" (1 Kings 18:24).

"... his name is the LORD—and rejoice before him" (Ps. 68:4).

"The fool says in his heart, 'There is no God'" (Ps. 14:1).

"They exchanged the truth of God for a lie, and worshiped and served created things rather than the Creator—who is forever praised. Amen. Because of this, God gave them over to shameful lusts" (Rom. 1:25–26).

"Then the LORD rained down burning sulfur on Sodom and Gomorrah—from the LORD out of the heavens" (Gen. 19:24).

"For he received honor and glory from God the Father" (2 Peter 1:17).

"Christ, who is God over all" (Rom. 9:5); "the Word was God" (John 1:1).

"... you have lied to the Holy Spirit.... You have not lied to men but to God" (Acts 5:3–4).

"... we wait for the blessed hope—the glorious appearing of our great God and Savior, Jesus Christ" (Titus 2:13).

"For in Christ all the fullness of the Deity lives in bodily form" (Col. 2:9).

---

[10]Elizabeth Ellis-Hagler, "George Met Jesus in the Charles Street Jail: The Bible in Human Transformation," *The Unitarian Universalist Christian* 44, no. 1 (Spring 1989): 7.

[11]Chworowsky and Raible, "What Is a Unitarian Universalist?" 265.

[12]Paul H. Beattie, "Personal Choice," in *Unitarian Universalist Views of God*, ed. Doris Hunter (Boston: Unitarian Universalist Association, n.d.), 9–10.

[13]John Sias from interviews with Rev. Steve Edington, *100 Questions that Non-Members Ask about Unitarian Universalism* (n.p.: Transition Publishing, 1994), 2–3.

[14]Chworowsky and Raible, "What Is a Unitarian Universalist?" 263–64.

[15]Paul Trudinger, "St. Paul: A Unitarian Universalist Christian?" *Faith and Freedom* 43 (Spring-Summer 1990): 57.

Jesus Christ

"... the world has many saviors."[16]	"Jesus answered, 'I am the way and the truth and the life. No one comes to the Father except through me'" (John 14:6).
	"Salvation is found in no one else, for there is no other name under heaven given to men by which we must be saved" (Acts 4:12).
"[Jesus was] a very special man, chosen to be indwelt by 'the Christ.'"[17]	"'You *are* the Christ, the Son of the living God'" (Matt. 16:16 [emphasis added]).
	"... he *is* Christ the Lord" (Luke 2:11 [emphasis added]).
"We do not believe that Jesus Christ was born of a virgin, performed miracles and was resurrected from death."[18]	"The virgin will be with child and will give birth to a son, and will call him Immanuel" (Isa. 7:14; cf. Matt. 1:23.)
	"The miracles I do in my Father's name speak for me" (John 10:25).
	"He is not here; he has risen, just as he said" (Matt. 28:6).
"In general, Unitarian Universalists ... honor the ethical leadership of Jesus without considering him to be their final religious authority."[19]	"There is a judge for the one who rejects me and does not accept my words; that very word which I spoke will condemn him at the last day" (John 12:48).
	(See also John 5:27; Acts 10:42; 17:31; 2 Timothy 4:1.)

---

[16]Tony Larsen, "Evangelizing Our Children," in *Salted with Fire: Unitarian Universalist Strategies for Sharing Faith and Growing Congregations,* ed. Scott W. Alexander (Boston: Skinner House, 1995), 128.

[17]Trudinger, "St. Paul: A Unitarian Universalist Christian?" 57.

[18]Sias, *100 Questions,* 3–4.

[19]Chworowsky and Raible, "What Is a Unitarian Universalist?" 263–64.

Man and Sin

"Come return to your place in the pews, and hear our heretical views: You were not born in sin so lift up your chin, you have only your dogmas to lose."[20]

"Unitarian Universalists reject the traditional Christian idea that the original sin of disobedience of Adam is inherited by all."[21]

"Potentially, the Divine Spirit is present in all human beings."[22]

"Many believe in a spirit of life or a power within themselves, which some choose to call God."[23]

"To be perfect is impossible. God forgives our imperfections because we were created that way. It's all right to be human."[24]

"Surely I was sinful at birth, sinful from the time my mother conceived me" (Ps. 51:5).

"For just as through the disobedience of the one man the many were made sinners, so also through the obedience of the one man the many will be made righteous" (Rom. 5:19).

"This is what the Sovereign LORD says: 'In the pride of your heart you say, "I am a god; I sit on the throne of a god in the heart of the seas."' But you are a man and not a god, though you think you are as wise as a god.... You will be but a man, not a god, in the hands of those who slay you" (Ezek. 28:2, 9b).

"I said, 'You are "gods"; you are all sons of the Most High.' But you will die like mere men" (Ps. 82:6–7).

"This only have I found: God made mankind upright, but men have gone in search of many schemes" (Eccl. 7:29).

---

[20]Sias, *100 Questions*, 1.

[21]Chworowsky and Raible, "What Is a Unitarian Universalist?" 267–68.

[22]Daniel G. Higgins, Jr., et al., *Unitarian Universalist Views of Jesus* (Boston: Unitarian Universalist Association, 1994).

[23]Sias, *100 Questions*, 2–3.

[24]John A. Buehrens, "Expectations," in *Our Chosen Faith: An Introduction to Unitarian Universalism*, eds. John A. Buehrens and F. Forrester Church (Boston: Beacon, 1989), 134, quoting Marjorie Newlin Leaming.

Salvation

"Rather than feel bound by human weaknesses and frailties, we emphasize human strengths. . . . You might call it a 'can do' religion."[25]

"Unitarian Universalism believes in 'salvation by character.'"[26]

". . . our moral fiber is equal to all demands."[27]

"It [Unitarianism] sees each as the child of God or, as many of us would say, as the child of the universe."[28]

Robert Fulghum, Unitarian minister and best-selling author, states, "We're all sons of God."[29]

"Unitarian Universalists reject the idea that God sacrificed Jesus 'His Son' to 'atone' for human 'sin.'"[30]

"The belief that Jesus atoned for the sins of the world by his death has little relevance for us."[31]

"Jesus did not think of himself as a Savior offering a blood atonement."[32]

". . . you were dead in your transgressions and sins" (Eph. 2:1).

"apart from me you can do nothing" (John 15:5b).

"If you, O LORD, kept a record of sins, O Lord, who could stand?" (Ps. 130:3).

"For it is by grace you have been saved, through faith—and this not from yourselves, it is the gift of God—not by works, so that no one can boast" (Eph. 2:8–9).

"For all have sinned and fall short of the glory of God" (Rom. 3:23).

". . . to those who believed in his name, he gave the right to become children of God" (John 1:12).

"You [unbelieving Pharisees] belong to your father, the devil" (John 8:44).

"Without the shedding of blood there is no forgiveness" (Heb. 9:22).

"Whom God hath set forth to be a propitiation through faith in his blood" (Rom. 3:25 KJV).

"In him we have redemption through his blood, the forgiveness of sins" (Eph. 1:7).

"The blood of Jesus, his Son, purifies us from every sin" (1 John 1:7).

(See also Revelation 1:5; 5:9.)

---

[25]Sias, *100 Questions*, 13.

[26]Marshall, *Challenge of a Liberal Faith*, 31.

[27]Ibid., 47.

[28]Ibid., 31.

[29]Religious News Service, "'Kindergarten' Writer Says Point Was Missed," *Los Angeles Times*, 21 December 1991, Orange County Edition, Special section, S-7.

[30]Chworowsky and Raible, "What Is a Unitarian Universalist?" 267–68.

[31]Sias, *100 Questions*, 21.

[32]Marshall, *Challenge of a Liberal Faith*, 229.

Heaven, Hell, and the Afterlife

"We simply do not know.... it is common to hear said, 'No one has ever returned to tell us about the afterlife.'"[33]

"There is enough hell in this world without creating an imaginary hell in another world."[34]

"[Unitarian Universalists] are concerned about this life, not an afterlife.... this natural world is the center of our lives."[35]

"We do not accept the idea of a physical resurrection."[36]

"After his suffering, he showed himself to these men and gave many convincing proofs that he was alive" (Acts 1:3).

"God has raised this Jesus to life, and we are all witnesses of the fact" (Acts 2:32).

"Then he will say to those on his left, 'Depart from me, you who are cursed, into the eternal fire prepared for the devil and his angels'" (Matt. 25:41).

"And the smoke of their torment rises for ever and ever" (Rev. 14:11).

"But seek first his kingdom and his righteousness, and all these things will be given to you as well" (Matt. 6:33).

"Do not store up for yourselves treasures on earth.... But store up for yourselves treasures in heaven" (Matt. 6:19–20a).

"Jesus answered them, 'Destroy this temple, and I will raise it again in three days....' But the temple he had spoken of was his body" (John 2:19, 21).

"Look at my hands and my feet. It is I myself! Touch me and see; a ghost does not have flesh and bones, as you see I have" (Luke 24:39).

"And after my skin has been destroyed, yet in my flesh I will see God; I myself will see him with my own eyes—I, and not another" (Job 19:26–27).

---

[33]George N. Marshall, "Unitarian Universalism," in *Encounters with Eternity: Religious Views of Death and Life After-Death*, eds. Christopher Jay Johnson and Marsha G. McGee (New York: Philosophical Library, 1986), 300. See also Johnson and McGee, "Appendix," in *Encounters with Eternity*, 325, 327.

[34]Marshall, *Challenge of a Liberal Faith*, 231.

[35]Ibid., 237.

[36]Sias, *100 Questions*, 21.

"What happens at the end of time and/or at a Judgment Day? . . . No one knows, but a loving God would not condemn any person to eternal damnation."[37]

"If you hear someone preaching hellfire and damnation. . . . chances are it's not a Unitarian Universalist!"[38]

"When it comes to a god who would condemn souls to hell, I'm an atheist. I can't believe in that kind of deity."[39]

"We believe that human beings should be accountable for their actions and make amends for any harm they may bring to others. But we don't believe that God will punish them."[40]

"No one 'goes' to hell; people create their own hells here on earth."[41]

"Reward and punishment are in this life, in the here and now."[42]

"But the cowardly, the unbelieving, the vile, the murderers, the sexually immoral, those who practice magic arts, the idolaters and all liars—their place will be in the fiery lake of burning sulfur" (Rev. 21:8).

"Then he will say to those on his left, 'Depart from me, you who are cursed, into the eternal fire prepared for the devil and his angels'" (Matt. 25:41).

"And the smoke of their torment rises for ever and ever" (Rev. 14:11).

"[God] will punish those who do not know God and do not obey the gospel of our Lord Jesus. They will be punished with everlasting destruction and shut out from the presence of the Lord and from the majesty of his power" (2 Thess. 1:7–9).

"Just as man is destined to die once, and after that to face judgment" (Heb. 9:27).

"If anyone's name was not found written in the book of life, he was thrown into the lake of fire" (Rev. 20:15).

---

[37]Johnson and McGee, "Appendix," 335, 338.

[38]William F. Schulz, "Our Faith," in *The Unitarian Universalist Pocket Guide,* ed. William F. Schulz, 2d ed. (Boston: Skinner House, 1993), 3.

[39]Tony Larsen with Ellen Schmidt, *A Catechism for Unitarian Universalists (Leader Guide)* (Boston: Unitarian Universalist Association, 1989), 5.

[40]Sias, *100 Questions,* 13.

[41]Johnson and McGee, "Appendix," 333, 335.

[42]Marshall, "Unitarian Universalism," 300.

Printed in the USA
CPSIA information can be obtained
at www.ICGtesting.com
LVHW030713050824
787165LV00011B/152

9 780310 488910